Jens Martin Gurr (ed.)
Norman M. Klein's "Bleeding Through: Layers of Los A

Urban Studies

Norman M. Klein, born in 1945, is professor in the School of Critical Studies at the California Institute of the Arts, and the author, for instance, of "The History of Forgetting: Los Angeles and the Erasure of Memory" (1997/2008) and "The Vatican to Vegas: The History of Special Effects" (2004), the multimedia historical novel, "The Imaginary 20th Century" (2016), "Freud in Coney Island and Other Tales" (2006). A critic, urban and media historian, and novelist, he has written extensively on the culture and politics of Los Angeles, on cinema, and on architecture.

Jens Martin Gurr, born in 1974, is a professor of British and Anglophone Literature and Culture at the University of Duisburg-Essen. He is co-founder and speaker of the Competence Field Metropolitan Research in the Universitätsallianz Ruhr (KoMet). His research areas include literary urban studies, theories and methods of urban and metropolitan research, model theory, literature and climate change as well as British literature of the 17th to the 21st centuries and contemporary US fiction.

Jens Martin Gurr (ed.)

Norman M. Klein's
"Bleeding Through: Layers of Los Angeles"

An Updated Edition 20 Years Later

[transcript]

With original texts from the 1st edition of Norman M. Klein's "Bleeding Through: Layers of Los Angeles 1920-1986" published by Hatje Cantz Publishers (2003).

The publication of this volume has been generously supported by the open access fund of the University of Duisburg-Essen administered by the University Library, by the University's Joint Center Urban Systems, and by the Dean's Office of the Faculty of Humanities of the University of Duisburg-Essen.

Bibliographic information published by the Deutsche Nationalbibliothek

The Deutsche Nationalbibliothek lists this publication in the Deutsche National-bibliografie; detailed bibliographic data are available in the Internet at http://dnb.d-nb.de

First published in 2023 by transcript Verlag, Bielefeld
© Jens Martin Gurr (ed.)

Cover layout: Kordula Röckenhaus, Bielefeld
Cover illustration: Overlay montage by Daniel Bläser

Print-ISBN 978-3-8376-6559-8
PDF-ISBN 978-3-8394-6559-2
https://doi.org/10.14361/9783839465592
ISSN of series: 2747-3619
eISSN of series: 2747-3635

Contents

Bleeding Through: 'The Making of'

0. Introduction

Norman M. Klein, Jens Martin Gurr

The reader of crime fiction is often a witness long after the fact, after the trail has gone cold. But the point is to reopen the case, look ironically for clues. It is a self-conscious conceit nowadays, to solve crimes, when media floods us with fake clues day and night. Where is the bottom to any crime? In the case of *Bleeding Through*, the reader lives in the year 1986 and makes friends with an elderly lady pushing ninety. The lady's name is Molly. She can often be seen shambling along, always a trifle off balance, up the hilly streets of Angelino Heights, a run-down older neighborhood in Los Angeles. The word out on Molly is that she murdered her second husband. And yet, she looks thoroughly unable to even raise her voice. Finally, the narrator asks Molly what happened to her second husband. She adjusts her jumbo eyeglasses, and answers simply: "His name was Walt, very different from my first husband, who sported with other women. Walt, to tell the truth, even in life, never left much of an impression."

In the original 2003 version, the print novella as well as interactive layers on a DVD delivered background about Molly, on what secrets she had; but as aporia, not enough to begin prosecuting her for murder. The reader chose from over a thousand images, voice-overs, videos, films, maps that both reveal and cloak her story. They reveal not only Molly's erasures, but also those of Los Angeles. Molly lives in the general downtown area, where more noir films were shot than anywhere else on earth. And yet, she hates crime movies, prefers screwball comedies.

In stages, we learn of Molly's seven final thoughts on earth. Tier I of the interface contours her thoughts into an archive of photos, films and voice overs. The sum of these feels almost like a novel or a movie. In Tier II, back stories, as research, to this potential Film Noir are revealed. By the Third Tier, we are too loaded down with information, as if the reader now knows too much even for a crime movie. This interface, designed by Rosemary Comella and Andreas Kratky, was released in 2002–2003, for the German media museum ZKM, in collaboration with the Labyrinth Media lab at the University of Southern California. It was based on a "docufable" from Norman Klein's *History of Forgetting* (1997), included as chapter 5 in the "Making of" section of the present book. Indeed, America's sense of crime has grown so much older since then.

Some 20 years after the first edition, this book includes the original novella, critical and historical essays on *Bleeding Through*, its contexts, its politics, and not least on changing perceptions of its aesthetic and medial strategies over time, as well as short fictions that went into the making of *Bleeding Through*. There are revaluations from different years, up to 2021, and an interview with Norman Klein. The sum of these reveal not only Molly's story, but the chronicle of what happened to downtown Los Angeles from 1920 to the present. The layers combine comic picaresque and documentary noir (and its hidden sources) as the comic embrace of the city itself.

As for the multimedia material contained on the DVD in the 2003 edition, this cannot simply be transferred to a website, now surely the expected option. More importantly, however, media evolution since 2003 suggests a different path anyway: While the interactive, non-linear hypertext interface requiring constant user activity was highly innovative then, and suited the enthusiasm about such media at the time, such interactivity has become far more normal (the award-winning interface as well as some reservations abouts its stochastic elements are discussed in Chapter 3 and in the interview in Chapter 9). In short, rather than seeking to replicate the 2003 experience of navigating the DVD[1], we present links to two documentary films on *Bleeding Through*. One is a documentary combining excerpts from *Bleeding Through* and footage of how the

---

1   Readers wishing to experience the original navigation may contact the editor to arrange for the sending of a USB device containing the original digital material.

interface is navigated[2], the other is the documentary *How to Make this into a Movie – Bleeding Through: Layers of Los Angeles 1920–1986* by two film students from the University of Duisburg-Essen, Lisa-Marie Krosse and Jan Niederprüm[3], which includes conversations with Norman Klein and Jens Gurr.

Chapter 1 of this book contains Norman Klein's original 37-page novella *Bleeding Through*, detailing Molly's story and highlighting the connection between urban development in LA through the 20th-century and Hollywood murder films. Chapter 2, "Montage and Superposition: The Poetics and Politics of Urban Memory in *Bleeding Through: Layers of Los Angeles, 1920–1986*" is a long essay on *Bleeding Through* by Jens Martin Gurr, while Chapter 3, "Spaces Between: Traveling Through Bleeds, Apertures, and Wormholes Inside the Database Novel" is an essay by Klein from 2007, which highlights his evolving views on the affordances and limitations of database novels such as *Bleeding Through*. In "Los Angeles since the End of Molly's Story: 1986–2021", which forms Chapter 4, Norman Klein traces some 35 years of urban transformation in Los Angeles to the present day, including thoughts on how COVID-19 may affect the city in the long run.

The 'Making of' section of the book opens with two short docufables from Klein's study *The History of Forgetting: Los Angeles and the Erasure of Memory* (1997) that were central to the genesis of *Bleeding Through*: Chapter 5, "The Unreliable Narrator", contains the kernel of Molly's story as later detailed in the novella "Bleeding Through", while Chapter 6, "Noir as the Ruins of the Left" is a docufable imagining what would have happened had Walter Benjamin survived his attempted escape from the Nazis and had settled in Los Angeles. Though never mentioned in *Bleeding Through*, Benjamin's views on the perception of cities are central to *Bleeding Through* and its conception of urban layers. Chapter 7, "The

---

2   The 44-minute film is to be found here: https://www.youtube.com/watch?v=d MX5xuuyIDQ.

3   The 21-minute film *How to Make this into a Movie – Bleeding Through: Layers of Los Angeles 1920–1986* is to be found here: https://www.youtube.com/watch?v=bt5 IVDBln5k.

Morgue: Fifty Ways to Murder a Man" is brief essay on a compilation of graphic newspaper reports on murders in Los Angeles that served as a backdrop to Molly's story, while Chapter 8, "Absences, Scripted Spaces and the Urban Imaginary: Unlikely Models for the City in the Twenty-First Century" is an essay written in 2002 in the early phase of working on *Bleeding Through*. With its discussion of urban polarities in Los Angeles and how they are both highlighted *and* glossed over in Hollywood films, but also with a discussion of American politics after 9/11, it provides key contexts for *Bleeding Through* and points forward to Klein's more explicit engagement with US politics in his later work. Chapter 9, a long interview with Norman Klein conducted for this volume in May 2022, focuses on the genesis of *Bleeding Through* and on the centrality of Walter Benjamin to its aesthetics and its politics of urban perception and representation. It thus seeks to tie together the key strands of this book.

We have decided not to modify, adapt or update the essays to express only present-day views; rather, apart from a harmonization of the reference system and the correction of obvious errors, they have deliberately remained unchanged: Written over a period of 20 years, they trace media evolutions and changing views on the strengths and limitations of multimedia database novels, including thoughts on how lessons learned from *Bleeding Through* came to shape Klein's second media novel, *The Imaginary 20th Century* (2016).

This book has long been in the making. In the words of Sterne's narrator Tristram Shandy (a shared obsession), we hope the reader will enjoy the roundabout evolution of a "slight acquaintance", begun in 2009 with an invitation to present *Bleeding Through* at a conference (for some reason, this did not work out), which – over more than ten years of intermittent though increasingly sustained conversation meandering around *Bleeding Through* – has "grow[n] into familiarity" and, in contrast to Tristram's relations with his readers, has "terminate[d] in friendship". If this result of our dialogue is only half as rewarding to readers as the dialogue itself has been to us, we will be most pleased.

Bleeding Through: Text and Contexts

1. *Bleeding Through*
The original novella from the 2003 first edition

Norman M. Klein

A very old lady ambles down a hill. A neighbor tells you that she may have murdered her second husband. You search for clues on her face, but it is unlined, as if she had kept it in storage. Molly is strangely cheerful in her dotage. If an event annoys her, she mentally deletes it. She has a genius for survival, that much is certain. She has outlived at least two husbands, along with her garment business downtown; she still opens for business after sixty years. You notice Molly's beaded purse. She has stored a pearl brooch inside, and a delicate gold chain, knotted up.

'I just don't look good in jewelry,' she explains.

While she smiles in your direction, she seems to be looking away at the same time. Molly is so used to practising an absent-minded guile, her eyes operate without her, like a ceiling fan running in an empty room. If she murdered her second husband, that would have been at least twenty-five years ago, in 1961. Of course, there is also a rumor that her husband hung himself up in her attic.

A pale hum rises from the Hollywood Freeway, three blocks below, down the hill. But once the wind shifts, it seems to blow the freeway north. Its hum grows louder, as it bounces off the canyon rim near Elysian Park. Directly overhead, the sky looks surprisingly clear, but that must be an illusion. Rumor has it that there is a bubble of oxygen here, because old folks go on forever. The breeze certainly is remarkably cool, and coming from the west. Somehow, it arrives from the ocean fifteen miles away. The hill must be faintly higher than the rest of the Basin, enough for a whisper of relief.

Looking in all directions, boxing the compass, dozens of houses have been torn down. But most of this neighborhood, Angelino Heights, is surprisingly intact; surely an accident, six square blocks sealed off in a double horseshoe. Some city maps even erase some of its side streets. But most of all, Angelino Heights has evolved into a hub of misinformation. You can count on facts that start here to get lost by the third person they reach.

By that time the rumors could raise the dead. They turn very ripe, ambient, even a trifle gothic. That is, if Angelino Heights could be called gothic. It certainly has claimed to be biblical. In the Teens, someone planted carob trees, after a trip to the Holy Land – St. John's bread, like in the Bible. They leave a vinegar sweetness on the ground. And a widower named Edgar suffered through a biblical revelation while restoring his Craftsman house. It wasn't voices, but something subtler when he was working on the roof.

Edgar gradually came to believe that he was not simply sanding down the alligator, and pouring a new foundation. He was in fact rebuilding the Holy City, for something like a second Temple. One day he simply changed his name from Ed to Ezra. He started memorizing Nehemiah in the Bible, on how to rebuild the walls of Jerusalem. He began to study the age of thousand-year-old redwood trees that in 1908 provided the four-by-fours for the foundation of his house. The numerology of fours is all over the Bible. He drilled a hole into the redwood, to feed electric cables; but miraculously, every bit broke. The redwood had turned to stone, like Nehemiah's walls of Jerusalem.

But Ed was definitely not consoled. The weight of being Ezra made him short of breath. He nearly slid off the roof hyperventilating. His hands swelled up with rheumatism, and he'd never been sick a day in his life. He gave bastard testimony, but no one was insulted or relieved to hear it.

Finally, Ezra settled in for the duration. He poured a new Western wall. He uncovered dead space hidden behind the kitchen, with papers left by a suspiciously unnamed group of people, mostly in very faint pencil, so no-one uninitiated could read them. Ezra also took endless coffee breaks. He found that caffeine helped his mind wander. He remembered dancing with his wife at dancehalls near downtown. His shoulders were still graceful. She was as light as a ghost even back then.

Molly used to visit and let Ezra serve her breakfast. Then she'd fold her hands, and face him down with a glazed look for as long as twenty minutes at a time, while he quoted this and that, mostly from Nehemiah. No matter how much his mind wandered, she answered him by smiling comfortably, as if she were waiting for him to decide what suit he wanted to order. She treated Ed like a customer, and it was a comfort to him.

Of course, it is well known among biblical scholars that the memoirs of Nehemiah are extremely unreliable. There is no telling how many storytellers and epochs are buried inside it, particularly since it is in the first person, most unusual in the Bible. I pointed that out to Ed or Ezra one day, and he agreed. Then he nodded gravely, as if I had stumbled onto a very deep truth, something only descendants of Aaron should be allowed to utter.

Men of Judah, he reminded me, are beginning to marry the women from Ashdod, Ammon and Moab. Half their children now speak the language of Ashdod, or even of other peoples; but not of Judah. Do not give your daughters to their sons, he warned me further, like the sons of Joiada, son of Eliashib, the high priest, son-in-law to Sanballat the Horonite – all driven away.

I was trying to figure out if this was some kind of covert anti-Semitism, but finally gave up. Sometimes, Ezra's eyes were so wide open, I felt I could see into the back of his head. So I asked him the question that had been gnawing at me for months now.

'You and Molly are old friends?'

'The oldest,' he said with a twinkle.

'You even knew her second husband.'

'Walt.'

'Where would he fit in the memoirs of Nehemiah, in the rebuilding of Jerusalem?'

I sensed my sarcasm. Maybe poor Ed sensed it too. I was momentarily heart-struck.

'Walt,' he said, 'was too organized for his own good. I meant to tell him that.'

'Where did Walt go?'

'Walt went the way he lived.'

'Which was?'

Omigod, I'd fallen into the trap.

'Too organized,' Ed/Ezra answered, having a laugh.

'Do you think the rumors are true?'

'About me?'

'No, that Walt disappeared in a mysterious way. There are rumors that he was perhaps murdered.'

'Or met a violent end. Probably, but he left with money for three, like the pharaohs of Egypt.'

'So he left alive, not murdered.'

'No, I couldn't say that for sure. Maybe you should ask Molly?'

'How can I do that?'

'True enough,' he agreed. 'I should have been there to console her back then. She wasn't altogether – how do you say? – she grew much prettier the older she got.'

'The last year she was around Walt, before he left with money for three, was she getting prettier?'

'That was a good period in the business for her, better than even I expected.'

So I left Ed to his regrets. The conversations with the other older folks went pretty much the same way, without the biblical qualities, much clearer, to the point, but the same way. Nevertheless, over the next eight months, I gathered what I could to assemble a story about Molly. There was definitely a story there, but what rhythm captured the best of it – that there were vast absences, and that these excited me much more than the facts themselves? There seemed no way to prove for or against the death of the dangerously organized Walt. The newspapers do not cover every corpse that shows up on the beach, or in a dump site near the train yards above downtown. And if a man simply vanished without a trace, in an organized way, there would be no newspapers there at all.

Walt probably did not have a funeral. He simply was lifted by an archangel, and taken out to sea. He left a daughter, Molly's stepdaughter, who looked gloomy and evasive every time I mentioned her father.

The stepdaughter, Nancy, was dutiful to Molly, as if she owed her a good day's work, at least until Molly turned senile. Then Nancy could attach her property. But Molly simply drifted along, pretending to forget her debtors, leaving the rent eternally low for the Mexican family downstairs. I've never seen a face so openly canny, but seemingly unaware of who was looking at her, or why.

As a result, I couldn't trust any of her stories. Not that her facts were wrong. Or that she didn't make an effort. Before each story, she would inhale deeply, to bring oxygen into her brain cells. Then she'd fog out dozens of key facts. Whenever I noticed, she would blow me off, smiling, and say, 'So I lose a few years.' Certainly, she lost the end of World War I – 1918 became 1922 instantly. Harding never died. For sixty years, she's covered up something very private about Mr. Julian, the oil swindler who bilked the city for millions in 1926; possibly his shirt size. Molly's loyalty to good customers was eternal. The Depression was 'mostly a problem of inventory.' Or: 'After Roosevelt was elected, they bombed Pearl Harbor.'

But there were seven memories in the years from 1920 to 1986 that were luminously detailed. Each was no longer than a day in length, but the day funneled into other material, eventually consumed her friends, her sister, her husbands. That night, I dreamed that I was given a mental function that could reverse the events of my life, like a switch on a toy train; or a function in a software program. I could shuffle the events simply by pulling the lever. That would fire up an engine made of flesh that gave me a small window of choice over how my so-called fate might work. In my dream, this felt like the illnesses that dogged many of the people closest to me, my anguish about failing to catch them as they were dying. In my dream, any of these events could not so much be reversed as re-edited for a different effect. The surprise events were like changes in fonts, or raw footage from a film.

The footage could be shot inside my head in high or low key, more or less contrasted. It was like deciding on your skin color. At the same time, the edited versions could feel like a pot cooking on the stove; but inside my five senses. I could make the events taste more like the dinner I had last night. Or make it blow like four AM in Los Angeles.

As I gradually felt my eyes needing to open, I turned toward my research on Molly's life, as if I could edit her sensations into a story that was symphonic in some way, or contrapuntal. I started to imagine scenes before her husband died as if from a camera, in quick time, or as photographs. I could write paragraphs about his last conversations with Molly – or someone else – but the words would have no sense of sight, as if I were moving Walt around by tapping the walls with a stick. I could gather data for Molly's story, and embed it like bots under the skin: newspaper clippings, historical photographs, and patches of interviews. Then I could assemble my assets into a vast database, for a search engine that could be selected according to the senses.

I felt a chill, as if I couldn't breathe properly. I woke up thinking my symptoms were partly about grief, as if I were watching my wife die slowly again, or was unable to comfort my family. My wife's breath had become so halted that she was preternatural. She was no longer able to eat or drink, because the cancer remained as the only part of her body that could be fed. She had ceased as an organism, and was only able to look up, and speak lovingly, but in denial, as if she were asking you to let her sculpt the last thought that she wanted to carry into oblivion.

That last thought is wafer-thin, and can be stored inside the sleeve of her small photo-album, a diary for a trip – if oblivion involves travel. Inside my head, not quite awake, I also begin editing my final thought. It too is wafer-thin, like a membrane, or a pig's ear. However, I choose my final thought badly, edit with the wrong software. My words are corrupted from third to first person, like Nehemiah's memoirs, or Molly losing a few years. In my dying breath, I was rude. Ghosts around the bed tried to be gracious, but looked at each other in a certain way.

So in my sleep I finally got a sense of how Edgar and Molly were feeling. They had to select the final thoughts that could be worn comfortably into oblivion. To get just the right angle, they tried every medium that they knew. And inside Angelino Heights, there were dozens to choose from, too many. Media extended like cilia from the body; they spread very thin, like the weather or micro-organisms, or wind patterns. They made forgetting simple, but a bit too dispersed, as simple as turning a switch or releasing a gas.

The reasons for all these force fields in Angelino Heights was obvious enough, nothing magical about that. The hill faces east toward an orbit of perhaps three square miles. Inside those three miles, under the skyline dropped by mistake into downtown ten years ago, more people have been murdered in classic Hollywood crime films than anywhere else on earth. Also inside the same three square miles, Angelino Heights faces an extreme of urban erasure. Hundreds of buildings gone: that could just as easily have been caused by carpet bombing, or a volcano erupting in the central business district.

To defend itself against the elements, Angelino Heights has turned to foster care. It takes in wounded buildings. More than a dozen have been delivered by truck from old neighborhoods undergoing wholesale bulldozing.

All these erasures leave absences. These absences, in turn, generate desire (as I'll explain later): cinematic misremembering, orphaned buildings and fake skylines – all crammed inside six streets that haven't changed physically since 1925. Together, they leave Angelino Heights mildly haunted, like a sour fragrance, or an insinuating ocean breeze from fifteen miles away. Many neighborhoods in LA are mildly haunted in this way – nothing very gothic really, except in the movies, where handheld cameras chase victims gunned down in slow-motion.

A truck pulls up suddenly in front of the house. My urban paranoia takes over. Thieves were coming to empty my place. But it was only the newspaper delivery at five AM. Then the light began to collect before dawn. I sat up, stared at the built-ins outlining the living room. In 1908, a carpenter would have been paid two dollars a day to install the woodwork. You showed him the picture in a pattern book, and he built it for you in less than a week. It was the era of pails of beer and sheet music.

But what does the standard of living before World War I mean to us today? Clearly, since the mid-Seventies we have been drifting in that dismal direction. We are leaving the century backwards, toward poverty as it was in 1908, toward a hierarchy just as ruthless. No wonder people want to live inside buildings with phantoms from that era, to help prepare their final thoughts for what Molly's sister, Nettie the Communist, used to call the big sendoff.

But for me this morning, the sendoff was still how to turn Molly's act of murder into a story. If it was murder, that is, if her second husband was actually run over by a milk truck in 1961; or eviscerated in Molly's kitchen, where he wouldn't stain the good furniture. Perhaps he jumped off City Hall, featured so prominently in LA films. There were certainly no traces of him now, in 1986. Only his absence was present; or in Molly's words, the way he wore out the lining of his sports jackets. Walt apparently never quite fit into human clothing. The shoulders usually hung on him as if he were part horse; so different from Molly's first husband, smiling Jack the 'sporting man.' Jack was always tailored, no matter whom he slept with, or how much he drank.

I try to visualize Molly arriving at the Santa Fe station in Los Angeles in 1920 or 1919, after the war. Under the glare of a much fiercer desert heat than today, she stared at the dust rising subtly at the train yards on Traction. She could smell ripe oranges on the ground blocks away, in groves to the east.

Molly was twenty-two, but as uncomfortable as a teenager with her body. She tried to evaporate into the background, but always failed. Even her eyes went from hazel to green, to whatever did not match the colors around her. Her hair was thick and almost red, Russian Jewish, and knotted in a bun. She liked to take oatmeal baths, mostly to avoid seeing her scrawny hips in the bath tub. She knew that she was not chaste though, because she liked to feel herself under the covers.

She had just lost her virginity to a roofer back in Indiana, one of the few Jews her age in the small town. He was barrel-chested, rather stout, named Archie because the sound faintly resembled his Hebrew name. Archie initiated what Molly liked to call her theory on burly men. It had something to do with the way a woman's hips and a burly man's thighs met. I took this to mean that Molly did not prefer the missionary position. I tried to put the question to her. She answered, 'The Jews don't seek converts.' I took that for a guarded yes.

Archie had a kind of rented charm. He affected the style of a man of means. Molly's father hated him, called him a bunco artist. Molly told her father to not call the kettle black. Who specialized in bunco more than her father, the burliest *gonnif* of them all? He clearly inspired her yen for well-dressed thieves. Her father used to sport a mink collar for business trips. He lost her mother's dowry in two years, presumably to buy penny stocks in Filipino oil, but the documents were lost in a flood.

Anyway, Archie nearly proposed to Molly more than once. Finally, he simply skipped town, to join the postwar building boom in Los Angeles. There, a few months later, near Brooklyn Avenue, he slipped off an East-lake roof and into a bay-fig tree. Molly sensed an opportunity. She wired Archie, who wired back. With her book-keeping degree from business school, she took the train to Los Angeles.

At the station, Archie wobbled on his cane to greet her. His face looked a trifle puffy, like a pastry soaked in brandy. And he was much too attentive. In the distance, Molly saw a short-waisted buxom woman wearing a brocaded georgette, with glycerine ostrich feathers in her hair.

'Who's that plump lady looking us over?' she asked.

'Katy, my second cousin.'

That was her first clue. Biblically speaking, second cousins do not breed cross-eyed idiots. And Katy had the bosom and accoutrements of a newly arrived immigrant – 'a winter storehouse,' Molly would say. But Katy probably could cook for hundreds, would do anything sexually that her lord and master asked, and undoubtedly had enough room to breed like bacteria. 'She's a hunky melon,' Molly told Archie. She laughed, but he only smiled.

What was even worse, Katy began to slim down a little over the next few months. Molly took to her bed, suffered unusually depressing men-strual cycles. Indeed, Archie was more than dividing his time. What to do? 'Should I throw in a subscription to the Saturday Evening Post? Boil up a side of beef? How about an athletic competition? We each lug in ten pounds of our secret lattke recipe?' Molly tried to be lighthearted about her predicament. But she soon noticed – as her first lesson in how to treat burly men – that dapper types like Archie preferred to make their own jokes, and hated her digs. No more needles about 'lord and master over the greenhorns.' And yet, try as she did to rein herself in, Molly felt her spleen grow larger, her acids build week by week. Stranger still, the more Archie grew distant, the more he slipped his hand down her skirts. But given the tradeoff, Molly decided, twice was enough for now. Once bitten, as the old story goes.

Meanwhile, she had settled into a rooming house near Brooklyn Avenue in Boyle Heights. She worked as a temporary bookkeeper; legend has it, according to her step-daughter, that she actually spent three weeks in the same office as Raymond Chandler, at Dabney Oil. Chandler looked very young, a little soft under the chin, and pretended that he came from England. That was all Molly remembered.

As for Brooklyn Avenue with its famous mix of Jews and Mexican, Japanese and other 'swart' young men, the *hamische* smells of herring barrels and the bins stuffed with soup greens only reminded her of Katy's cooking. She became self-conscious about the narrowness of her hips. The men leered anyway. To be practical, however, Molly started to keep an eye out on Sunday afternoons. Sure Archie was well-spoken, and had a mopey sadness that appealed to her, but he was all but spoken for. The uneducated melon had won.

Molly let herself cry for three days, even missed a day of work. Then she decided that she had to cross First Street to downtown. As she walked far beyond the river, the haze made by the heat was intense. Yet even on the asphalt streets, between the bank buildings on Spring, the topsoil from orchards would sometimes blow tiny grains of dirt into your teeth. There were stories that the hot California sun could fade the color of your eyes.

She refused to take the trolley today, wandered gloomily, sat under a date tree in the Central Park that was not much of a central park. The so-called crimson veil of the desert sunset was so soothing that she fell in love with the early evening in LA, came back four nights in a row to think. There was no point writing to her mother, who was still recovering from what the Cossacks did to her own mother fifty years ago.

Central Park, soon to be called Pershing Square, was a bughouse square with speeches by radicals of every lost cause, with tottering old men, with women's clubs whose members would gather at the benches before going to concerts at the symphony hall across the street. Molly finessed her way into the group. The music went in one ear and out the other.

She went to a dry-goods store to get some stockings. There a flirtatious young man waved her over. His nails were magnificently trimmed and lacquered. While he said his piece about getting lost in her eyes, which were unfortunately turning that strange green again, he opened a box of European nylons. Like a button loose on his fly, he slid his fingers through the nylons, turning his wrists like a fish. As he stiffened the nylons and made gestures with them, Molly got the point. She even got faintly wet, very faintly.

This was the first sexual kindness from a stranger in weeks now, since Archie had begun to try Katy's full menu. It was then she decided to go into men's clothing. Surely that was a sensible line to get attention, and make one's way.

Then there is one of those gaps. For the duration of a month, something embarrassing brought Molly into the men's apparel business. It may have been a salesman, a reason to be hired. After all, she was on her last legs. One fact is clear: by May 1921, Molly was an expert on male etiquette, on how to make the famous first impression. She had learned the importance of wearing freshly laundered white shirt waists with simple dark suits. The smell of soap was obviously erotic to men.

But perfect diction was the most erotic of all. 'Beneath a ragged coat,' she would say, 'there may beat an honest heart.' That was one of her best opening lines. The tone was crucial. It had to be delivered naively, as if she'd just memorized it from a book. Then she usually followed with, 'A bright intellect,' – shy smile ('like yourself') – 'might even rise above the bright checked suit and yellow tie.'

'But there are better guarantees, of course. Something casual but appropriate.' Then she would 'accidentally' brush shoulders against the customer; pretend that she hadn't felt him; and reach down to gather a bolt of fabric. 'Those guarantees, as you well know,' – a shy, empathetic glance – 'give a man that ... first impression.'

Then she would slowly massage the fabric from below. If the customer was still smiling like a puffed toad, she could probe further. He was halfway there. She might ask about his business, his children. Did he really like the prevailing cut? Did he ever – now be honest – have the slightest need for a cutaway? Anyway, this wool would never do for a costume that … formal. 'I agree with you, an intelligent man does best with a simple business suit.'

In the late afternoons, she would do the books. The owner Ike – for Isaac – was fidgety about her at first. It became quite apparent to her that there were two books. The second worried Ike the most, what he called 'the excise.' Molly was instructed to jointly and severally pay his friends for excise. This excise came from overseas, but was apparently not liquor. It was service added. Ike never told her what excise looked like, whether you wore it, mounted it, swallowed it internally.

Ike would study her face when she did the books, the excise in particular. In time, almost in self-defense, she began to study his back. His eyes tended to be shrouded. He barely slept. Apparently, his wife's ghost used to visit him in the evening, and he would pretend to play a game of five hundred with her.

Excise helped relieve Ike's losses. Hundreds of his customers were invested in it, for value received. Perhaps excise was a kind of barter. She wrote, in rapid business writing: 'I hereby covenant and agree that George T. Hoar be fitted for two cutaways, and one afternoon tweed. We will also sell and convey the following from his haberdasher, an *excise* to be withdrawn from the capital sum of four hundred and eighteen dollars.'

One afternoon, while Molly was about to test out a new erotic sales pitch based on books of etiquette she had memorized earlier that week, the owner literally pulled her aside. This was at least the fourth time he had pulled her in that way. She all but felt his bull neck breathing on her, the way he did when he leaned like drapes over her shoulder to read her columns, the excise. To appease that breathing, she used to leave a few random curls unfastened toward her back. Given her limited means, just a room in Boyle Heights, there was no point taking anyone for granted. Ike (or Isaac in his loneliness) was definitely a man of experience, even if he did spend evenings at home playing cards with his dead wife.

Today, Ike asked Molly to join him on a trip, to leave the showroom, and not worry about the receipts. Time or providence would take care of them for now. He wanted to drive her somewhere very important, west of the city, bring her one step deeper inside his business. As they left the store, she noticed in a fitting mirror that her eyes had turned that ugly green again.

Ike (more than Isaac) liked to gamble. For some strange reason, he drove Molly up North Broadway, pointed out the Italian card parlors and bookies. Then he began to confess to her, occasionally taking her hand as he worked the clutch. 'I get the point,' Molly explained. 'I learned how to drive back in Indiana.'

Then he told Molly about his swashbuckling days. Molly wondered if half of it were true: At age fifteen – that looked to be about forty years ago – Isaac as Ike was taught to gamble, and to steal fruit in Chinatown. A hasher used to sneak him to "N* Alley" ("Calle de los Negros")[1] after work. It was remnant Mexico: hardpacked earth everywhere, adobes, weary hotels. Hatchet men from the tongs looked straight out of a dime novel. He saw teenage girls sold for $ 200 and up.

Sold for what, rented for what, Molly asked? Isaac explained with euphemisms so vague, Molly could barely decipher a word. Apparently, Ike knew chink whores and Mex whores – an eager young boy. Sadly, Ike found them a vast improvement on his fiancee, a drab third cousin with Prussian Jewish manners, a pouty look of exhaustion on her face. So he angled for a way to cancel the engagement. Finally he told her that he hoped he didn't carry a disease. The girl cried to her mother, and news spread.

Young Isaac's parents felt obligated to bring him in to the rabbi for guidance. They left him alone with the holy man at the Base Hamigdash. For five minutes, Isaac was required to sit still, and watch the rabbi

---

1   2022: That term was used regularly in turn-of-the-century Los Angeles daily speech. It was even on various maps. It indicates a racist overlay that is crucial to understanding the history of the city, especially during that earlier period, but with deep importance later on. As a deep irony, that slim alley north of the plaza was not a black neighborhood. Most of the residents were Chinese and Mexican. In other words, Chinese and Mexicans were also freely designated in that racist "non-white" way. Moreover, the area was policed and zoned in a deliberately racist fashion.

complete a prayer. In the middle, the rabbi shared a smile with a ghost over young Isaac's shoulder. The ghost apparently was smiling back from the small orange-pebbled window. Then the rabbi began adjusting his tephillin.

Ike stared at the window, and started to get anxious. To break the ice, Ike made a crude joke about the Queen of Sheba's ass, in so many words. The rabbi stared back glumly. I have an answer to that story, he explained. The rabbi moistened his finger, then thumbed through the Talmud. Finally, he rattled something in Hebrew, but as always he never translated the same passage the same way twice:

There was a young woman of Judah, he began, breaking off to re-read the commentary on the commentary. Her hair was lustrous. Her eyes were like moonlight. But she was pale and sick with guilt. The holy teacher could sense that her body had been awakened. 'Your holiness,' she said, 'I have slept with a married man.'

His holiness, amazingly enough, had in translation exactly the same personality as the rabbi. According to the Talmud, the holy teacher waited for the girl to stop weeping. Gradually, he made her look at him and said, 'When you accidentally dip your fingers in honey, what do you do?'

Isaac was impressed: Was this an exact translation? Then, in so many words, Ike wondered out loud if rabbis ever dip the honey. The holy man laughed, but didn't say no. So the boy felt even more confused; but much better. This was, in fact, the closest Ike (or Isaac) ever came to joining any organized religion. 'I realized that it makes more sense if you're selling God than if you're buying. But in my business, you're selling to gentiles.'

Finally Ike married a Protestant girl. He decided to cut off from his family altogether, even from relatives back east. Every Friday, his mother would light the Yortzeit candles, and call his name, as if he were dead. Only right before she died did she forgive Ike, since he had become so rich and had, as Isaac, bought new windows for the synagogue. Ike used his wife's money to buy a small factory as well. At the brass-fitted showroom on Broadway, Ike sold to anyone no matter what Messiah they believed in. Criminals with good manners were fine. Whether the money came from their shoe or the bank, be they Moluccas with tattooed necks or the King of Panama – he could fit them.

After a suit was ready, Ike always took the paying customer drinking and gambling; sometimes on Spring Street, sometimes in Ocean Park. Ike the owner saw himself as a sporting man, even though he lost the taste for it in his forties when his wife grew ill. She turned to spiritualism, and Ike turned to the burlesques on Main Street (but only to watch). However, as she weakened and started to die, Isaac suddenly learned to see through her eyes. Like that strange rabbi, he began to communicate with ghosts at the window. Then, while his wife shrank for a year in bed, Isaac let her ghosts advise him in business. Their advice was never quite right for the season, but they obviously had a good eye for the long term.

Then, after his wife died, jealous to the end that he was still alive, she sent all the other ghosts away. So Ike has grown lonelier. He no longer can speak his mind, not even (and especially not) to his son. Having lost even the taste for gambling, he can no longer relax. He wakes up at three in the morning, spends hours listening for whispers, hoping to be haunted again, and finally goes to the showroom at sunrise. In recent months, Isaac has begun to wait, almost impatiently, for something from Molly, the homely, oddly appealing, skinny Jewish girl, with the long sad face. He watches her recite from Eichler's new book of etiquette. He inhales her quietly, secretly, while she keeps his books in the late afternoon.

Isaac glances at Molly for reactions to all this. He drives her up Glendale, past Edendale. One of Sennett's revolving stages is being torn down. Ike points out that above Sennett's movie stages, the dairies and the horse ranches are disappearing. He keeps waiting for her to speak more. They drive south into the old Los Angeles oil field. Scattered flimsy wooden derricks, survivors of the hundreds there at the turn of the century, stand on the slope with dwellings encroaching upon them. The air is faintly acrid, like vinegar.

Then Ike drives toward lemon groves further west, and up the foothills through purple verbena. They head south of the walnut orchards; he points toward olive trees being tended. New gaps are opening quickly, the start of a housing boom. Construction crews, whites, Mex, Japs, Filipino, are frying in the sun. They go six long days a week, from can't to can't, the owner says (an old plantation phrase he heard some-where), with checks every Saturday morning. But most of all, there are miles upon miles of open fields and unpaved drainage ditches. The shiny rails of track can be almost blinding for interurban red cars. The horns of the red cars moan, while the horns of the yellow cars gong. Inside the business core, just five or six blocks running south on Broadway from First Street, trestles for streetcars crackle and shiver into the second store windows.

Suddenly, Isaac looks so worn that Molly advises him to remove his jacket. While they stop, he asks her if an older man needs a daughter, or needs a wife. Molly told him that she would take a few days to decide.

A year later, when Molly was married to his son Jack – as much mar-ried, that is, as that restless boy could be – Isaac offered advice. Jack sat back pretending to listen, the usual blank attitude, as if he were in a box at a theater.

Isaac said, 'My son has inherited his father's weaknesses, and his mother's regrets.'

Then Ike brushed against Molly, and looked hungrily at her hair. 'But I never saw a young man who understood my story about honey any better than Jack.'

Jack saw a very different city when he drove Molly around, especially after the old man died so strangely, and left those excises unexplained and entirely on Molly's shoulders to figure out. By 1924, the boom had begun to subside. But there were billboards everywhere. Men would re-lieve themselves under a billboard, while the wife would stand by the car and look away demurely. From Canada and Mexico, trucks came in with tarpaulins laced down tightly; inside them booze for Jack's friends who needed a handsome suit.

He agreed with Molly that he couldn't sleep comfortably in the house anymore, that they should leave Bunker Hill before the ghosts took over every window. They already were making a racket. Jack wondered if his mother was still able to stop his father from speaking to ghosts; and if a few of them might leave some business advice for the long term.

Jack was convinced that jacket lapels with silk were a good invest-ment. Molly had a habit of putting her hand on his thigh, to check if he was skittish or spent, he thought. There was a story he liked to tell her about a friend of his who put down two shotguns as a down payment on a house. But he rarely brought these friends over, especially after Molly moved on to Angelino Heights.

Jack clearly had his own gin-soaked theories on gracious living. He devoted thirty years to the study of his declining health, as if it were a stock exchange. He remembered seeing, as a child, his father talking to white-robed Klansmen riding horses across downtown to the auditorium on Olive to see *Birth of a Nation* in 1915.

The problem was essentially this: His father had started in a store on Main Street, a small factory. Then came the showroom on Broadway. He found a partner, with gambling connections in Chinatown (or perhaps in Little Italy on North Broadway, up above Dog Town). The partner was a leech in the end, so his father paid him off. But Jack still enjoyed spending time with the leech's family, and the leeches who were their friends. Thus, despite all the Protestant affect, his father wound up a kike; while Jack was a swank with an edge. His father was always poor; Jack was always rich. His father knew how to dry up. Jack always said the wrong thing at the right time. But it was a gruesome shock the way the old man went up in flames.

Molly was pleased to know that Gloria Swanson started in Chicago, and would marry royalty next. It was clear to her that Wallace Beery, Swanson's first husband (she was on to her third) vaguely resembled every man who sniffs up a fifteen-year-old's dress; and waits like a ghoul, even for years. She was mildly thrilled to overhear a customer saying that Gloria wore her dresses 'too thin.'

It kept Molly going just to know that Gloria Swanson had rented – and been beaten by her first husband – just down the block back. Of course, that would have been 1916 or 1918, before Molly came to Angelino Heights. Finally, in 1923, Molly actually met and passed ten words with tiny Gloria while she was visiting her old haunt.

Years later, Archie, who never quite recovered from falling off a roof – and wasn't much of a catch after all – suddenly moved near Molly. He offered himself and his miseries on the rebound. Failing that, he tried to show off a little. 'I haven't seen Gloria Swanson since she was sixteen

years old,' he said. 'She had the tiniest feet, like a little dwarf child.' Maybe
so, Molly answered, but in 1924 Gloria made more money than any man
in her business, on earth.

Molly's taste for movies ended when her career went sour. Molly
never much cared for anything but comedies anyway. She mostly went
to see the cut of the suits. But I had to interrupt her stories this one
time: Did she know, I told her excitedly, that in the three square miles
around where she worked and went home, more people were murdered
in classic films than anywhere else on earth?

No, she hadn't the first clue, never saw anything of it. I thought I was
doing something important by showing her movie stills from *Double In-
demnity*, *DOA*, *Chinatown* (a murder just a block from her house, only a
few years ago), *T-Men*, *Crimson Kimono* ... The stack spilled out of my lap.
I reached to scoop up the stills.

'I knew men who committed murder,' she interrupted suddenly.
'Three men to be exact. But I don't want their ghosts coming back to slug
me, because I told.' Then she peered vaguely through those beer-bottle
glasses. I never could tell if she was pulling my leg.

I told her how many movies were shot in Echo Park Lake, where she
used to sit under those shady and ornamental trees on a Saturday. She
saw quite a mix: Russian Jews, Mex, anarchists, Nazarines from the Four
Square Gospel. She especially liked the Egyptian papyrus and water lilies
growing in the shallows, where waterfowl – swans, ducks, coots, grebes
and geese – would come for shelter at different times. But the lake is such
a tiny patch, only eight acres, barely four feet deep. Lately, they dredged
it, found wedding rings, china plates, bottles for anything from poison
to elixirs and soft drinks. The river dribbled down Glendale originally.
And the lake was simply an artificial pond, built to power a woolen mill
at Sixth and Pearl (now Figueroa).

Molly knew about the woolen mill, but not the murders in the
movies. She had watched the Mex take over the Lake, but they never
bothered her. In 1943, she saw blood on a store window after the Zoot
Suit Riots. She knew about dinges, the Watts Rebellion, and sixty years
of hop, one kind of social trauma or the other. Mexicans were swart
and bronze faced. During the war, blacks turned the abandoned Little

Tokyo into Bronzeville. Like everyone else, she called it Bronzeville, didn't worry much about what happened to the Japs, the Nips, the little Japanese. She was a specter with an attitude. As with most of us, her problems sealed her off from the rest.

A man two blocks away spends five years building a fall-out shelter, a Simon Rodia (Watt's Towers) in reverse; another case of someone haunted by his wife's disappearance.

A friend of Archie's gets so drunk one day that he falls into a bus and dies. His children turn into thieves. The basement is piled high with car batteries. The plumbing implodes. The electricity dangles and pops from light fixtures. Their mother finally sells the house. The children spill in all directions. But each one has the same dream: the house walks into their head, and tells them to never move back.

Archie certainly damaged Molly's theories on burly men. So, as a corrective, she took a fancy to slight men for a few years, had a yearning for an Alsatian chef who owned the big Florentine house on Douglas. She told him that with some exercise, he wouldn't look so gaunt. Then before much more could be said, the chef had a stroke; and installed an electric chair on a rail to take him to the second floor.

Worse still, a slight man at a rooming house on Boston Street in Angelino Heights kidnaped a ten-year-old girl. Then he held her for ransom, stirred headlines for a week, collected the money; but had already tortured and slaughtered her. Molly actually remembers seeing his hollow, gentle face on Carroll Avenue that very week. They were passing each other slowly, near a large bay-fig tree, below Mr. Pinney's house. An ice-cream truck was jingling behind them. Like in a romance novel their eyes met. They each said hello. She smiled, kept looking, to drop a hint, maybe lay some groundwork. He was cordial, a bit lost in his thoughts.

'When it came to romance, I never had a good sense of timing,' she said. In 1927, Jack disappeared for two days. He came back like a Viking on a death barge. He was literally too tired to make excuses. That was Jack. So Molly didn't even ask where he went, only if he planned to go back regularly. Molly slaps her forehead: 'I never had that presence of mind with men. My sister Nettie had that and more. Of course, she always chose badly.' She paused, then added, 'Walt, my second husband, always said he loved me for my sense of timing.'

She didn't say Walt my ex, or Walt who died of natural causes. Then Molly laughed loudly, almost a cackle. Walt was one of her successes. Her 'timing' with him had finally worked out. Next day, I went to a newspaper morgue, looking for articles on Walt's disappearance. Instead, I found fifty ways to kill a man between 1959 and 1961 (along with five suicides). I've scanned all the articles into a database for you: the 'sluggings,' the bodies dumped in olive groves, in the bushes, in vacant lots, hotels, railroad yards, at the Long Beach Recreational Center. The deadly argument between 'an invalid and his friend.' The 'wheelchair man' who kills his estranged wife in a duel. The police chief's son who keeps confessing that he stabbed someone. The quarrels in parking lots. The famous last words: 'Go ahead and shoot.'

The short stocky gunman with a quick temper. The chivalrous man who is shot dead while trying to stop a 'burly' robber from pistol-whipping a woman. The discarded husband who kicks down the back door of 'the house that was once his,' but is fatally shot by his successor, who says, 'If my wife wanted you, she would go back to you.' The boyfriend who shoots the husband while the wife watches. The head carried in a bag by a 'bowling bum.'

The man slain in a row over cutting his lawn. The Disneyland Hotel Scene Killing. The Wild West Bandits Slayings. The coffee-shop owner who shoots a troublemaker. The poisoned cocktail killer. The missing gun in the murder of a 'Hollywood doctor.' The man who for months makes advances toward another man's wife, only to be continually rebuffed. So he borrows a gun – for 'target practice' – from someone in the office at Columbia Records, and kills her husband. In another musical murder, a 'musician cafe owner' is shot in 'a bedroom pistol duel.' The murders blur into each other.

A man eating a hotdog is berated by a stranger, then 'mysteriously' shot. An unidentified car drives backward and forward over a husband's body. A wife tells police: 'I honestly thought there were no bullets in the gun, it fired and misfired so often.'

We are bizarrely charmed by the comedy of murder. Crime story takes us farther from the intense realities of a person's life toward a hypnogogic escape, extremely vivid but somehow medicated, easy on the nerves.

So many of these murders feature domestic partners. The story turns into a dark sexual farce about forensic detail:

- Points of entry – for the bullet, the adulterer, or the assailant;
- Time of murder – the last time, the first time, the best time, her time of the month, his bad timing;
- Vengeance – cradling his hunting rifle under her arm, she listened by the window outside their house for the grunting of her bare-assed husband;
- Amnesia – the murderer has forgotten where he was that night.

The photos that go with these clippings cut out their surroundings. Often, editors have them cropped in white before they are printed. And no matter how graphic the police photo – the bullet through the eye, the blood on the couch – it is a mode of erasure. Among police photos, I find what should be Walt's body. He lies under a blanket on a cement embankment of the LA River, just north of downtown. Four exhausted men stare in confusion. Then I discover that on the same day, the downtown editor canceled photos about racist crimes, particularly the railroading of blacks and Latinos. He went with the nameless crime instead.

I gather my research into boxes, perhaps as a back story for a screenplay. But no matter how 'realistic' I make it, the screenplay reverts into a mode of erasure, an allegory about psychotic vendettas and petty greeds – in a world where all crooks are in business, and all businessmen are crooks. I guess LA murder has a distinct fragrance. And this fragrance plays into the longstanding American distrust of urban democracy. Many Americans believe, as they did in Jefferson's day, that equality can survive only in a small town. By contrast, fascism flourishes in crowds. Murder becomes a call for order, and a symptom of alienation. Of course, I absolutely do not believe these noir fantasies. I prefer to make Walt's murder a critique of urban capitalism; but then the crime becomes a defense of the suburbs.

And yet, these neutralizing murder stories have brought me closer to who Molly was. I now enjoy the same evacuated indifference that she does. On a buffet in her dining room, next to china cabinets imploding with depression glass, I find a photograph of her from 1959. Her face had blossomed by then. The camera almost finds planes on her face, and a bone structure. But her expression looks much the same: surprised to be there. She is walking toward the bank on Spring Street, to gather pay vouchers for her factory workers. The investment houses near the bank have hired men to polish the brass on the fire hydrants. But the postwar decay has begun to show. Molly chats with prostitutes and secretaries who literally share the same street – makes girl talk. But thinking back in 1986, she imagines that she was raising feminine consciousness all around her. These brief conversations, with her payroll sack in one hand, were the only ones she ever had with whores, and have thus been inflated in her mind's eye. 'My memory plays tricks,' she admits.

We live as tourists, but remember as if we were in the thick of things. Yet despite our mental evasions (my own in particular, after my girlfriend's boyfriend robbed me blind), we clearly belong to every square foot around us. That should be my story, not the fifty murders condensed into one screenplay, or one novel. But first, I must gather enough evidence. Probably the gathering is richer than the telling anyway.

The story would go something like this: Molly undoubtedly murdered her second husband. But she couldn't murder a soul. When she arrived in Los Angeles, soon after World War I in either 1919 or 1920, she already had something to hide, since she never contacted her family again. Coincidentally, she married into a family that ignored its relatives in much the same way. She clearly had customers who went to jail, probably committed murders, or ordered them. She also had customers whose only crime was using a stamp more than once, or never mentioning at tax time how much they made on their saving accounts.

She is protecting the ghosts that hover around her. She has lost the ability to distinguish between sunrise and sunset. Her stepdaughter and the family of her sister Nettie all need money. The Mexicans renting from Molly treat her like the only roof over their heads. Then there is Archie, the alcoholic roofer who finally moved near her, after losing his fat Russian wife. But Archie cannot even make his way to his back door at night, and is under the care of his sister. And she is falling apart, won't be around much longer. I hear Archie sleeping in his backyard tonight. His snoring wakes up the dogs for blocks around.

Unreliable Narrators

It is time to unravel or commit literary murder. I am now convinced that Molly had Walt murdered in 1959. He hasn't been heard of or seen since. Molly, of course, never says otherwise. She likes being unreliable. Narrators don't get much more inscrutable. And her stepdaughter, Walt's own flesh and blood, is an outright liar.

Molly's motives won't help me much. Every motive imaginable has led to murder at some time. In 1959, Walt and Molly argued until the wallpaper began to peel in the kitchen. He tried to beat her, even stab her, but wasn't in shape, hadn't lifted anything more than a shoebox in twenty-five years. Also, Walt suddenly had begun to smell old, like her father. He was a huckster, a liar, a schizophrenic. He was a thief who rummaged through her savings, and planned to sell off her factory. He went with prostitutes from Fifth and Spring who told Molly he wasn't much. He was in league with the devil, with the gentiles, with the communists, with the neo-nazis, with a masonic order who saw themselves as ancient Spartans, and believed that homosexuality could save the British Empire. His sour disposition infected everyone around him like a rash. He began to collect guns, would store them like fine china in the living room. He was so schizoid that he annoyed the ghosts who visited regularly from the attic. He found out Molly's darkest secret, and threatened to expose her. Since we don't know that secret, she must have done away with him. Walt lived in a blind rage. He intentionally left his fly open at the office, to keep everyone amused. He was too frail from cancer, too kind to have to suffer.

Or simply put: Molly had had enough. She believed that what you don't know can't hurt you.

Have I hit a motive that is convincing yet? It is a daunting prospect to give up all those newspaper clippings in order to make this story legible. Perhaps I am too reliable to be a narrator. I promise to murder him off as much as the evidence will allow. I have about a thousand photographs and newspaper articles, over two hundred relevant movies on file, and over twenty interviews, along with hours of interviews with Norman Klein; and hundreds of pages of text. With all of these elegantly assembled in a DVD-ROM, I can follow Laurence Sterne's advice (1760): to make an entertainment, a tristful *paideia*, a mocking of the truth. I can draw her 'character … merely from (her) evacuations.'

So we begin by locating Molly in noir flashback. However, the grammar of noir is built around racist and sexist egoism, mostly a white male tradition: what I call 'white men caught in the wrong neighborhood.' It has been adjusted in recent decades – more female noir novelists, more black, Latino, Chinese, and Japanese noir; and noir from every sexual persuasion. But fundamentally, the point of view that gives these sinister tales their ferocity will not do here.

Molly simply was not a noir heroine. I call her Molly of no bloom, the Emma of Angelino Heights. She is a Eurydice who adjusted quite well to spending half the year in the underworld. She learned how to dress for it, found the best, cheap restaurants. She was vaguely corruptible, like most unreliable interviews I have known. Perhaps I should make her a female version of Uncle Toby (from *Tristram Shandy*, 1759, the dotty man with a hobby-horse, and a gift for forgetting most things). That is, if Toby ever hired assassins to kill his wife.

Molly is as genial as Uncle Toby, but much cannier, not a cheerful old fool blathering on about a groin injury from the 1695 Siege of Namur. Suppose Toby as Molly lived in Angelino Heights? Where do we go from there? Toby has a blackout. She wakes up with a corpse in the dining room. It sits, shoulders dangling, as if waiting for breakfast waffles. Toby has 'a killer inside her,' a touch of Jim Thompson, but too pathological for Molly.

Molly tried a therapist once, when it was the fashion. He was a customer, seemed well-read, knew his tweeds. She spent three months talking about her parents, and her legs, her pride and joy. She even discovered a well of resentments inside. And luckily, the sessions were paid off in trade. But it was clear that the therapist was deeply unhappy with his own marriage, and had never honestly wanted to go into medicine, did it to please his immigrant parents.

Finally, Molly wasn't sure who was helping whom. She felt somewhat better, but finding the right man, even pretending to find the right man, seemed like the best therapy. That was her quixotic search, a picaresque where no one was ever on the road. I imagine the devil offering her a Faustian deal, but she refuses because she thinks he's angling to get her to Palm Springs, to sell her time shares in a condominium. Molly prided herself on never carrying more than you need; except, of course, for the jewelry she kept in her beaded purse: her dowry, as you will discover later on.

I need a different model for the unreliable narrator as well as for the fragrant noir world, vital though these have been for modern literature, detective stories, cinema suspense; and for lies the State Department delivered on broadcast news during the Cold War. (This is 1986, remember. You the reader may have more grisly forms of unreliable news to deal with.)

I believe that the unreliable narrator is an absence, like a chiaroscuro. The absence is a camera, an aperture. Beyond the frame of this aperture lies something more interesting than the answer to a crime. Answers are so formal, so mechanical, like bad television murders: all the world put back in order inside twenty-two minutes.

This aperture generates desire more than action: the unspent eroticism when a stranger you can never meet accidentally looks exciting; the ache when children fail to love their parents, are politely dismissive; the anamorphic gaze, the yearning across the room that is never returned (he was looking at someone behind you instead). Absence is a lingering distress that is deeply pleasurable; and truer to the way we actually live than a corpse dropped on the lawn. It is the trace left by a crime, the erasure and forgetting of a crime.

Let's toss Walt on the tracks. We don't even care how he got there, not for the moment. It is suspense, after all. Perhaps he was dumped on a concrete river embankment, as in dozens of police photos that I have seen.

We check for clues, in all four points of the compass. Clearly, we want to know more than what happened to poor Walt (even if he got what he deserved). What possessed Molly? Or even who possesses Molly? Did her legs finally hold up after all? Did the 'good-natured horse face', as Walt liked to call her, finally learn to kick?

I prefer to set the aperture wider, around the criminal misremembering of the city of LA itself, more Balzacian, give it the sweep that monstrous crimes deserve. There are numerous characters in the background who may show up, but certainly will appear in future volumes of *The History of Forgetting*. Harry Brown is a lawyer who orders a leisure suit in 1928. But he is in a very strange line of work (as I will show later on). His files, and the worm-eaten young scholar who tends to them, present an alternative history of the city that never arrives, only leaves its traces.

For example: A man decides to quit the 500 rummy game at home along with the droll anomie of watching to see if the dog's tail will light up because the dog always sleeps too close to the fireplace. He leaves his sprawling bungalow, and the ornamental trees and the Japanese garden on nearly an acre setback, in order to get some smokes: like Jack leaving Molly for 'some air in the country, before they drop another house on it.' Three hours later, or in Jack's case two days later, the man returns. The man has a box of cigars in his jacket pocket (that is, if the cigars are indeed just a cigar). Where did he go? He looks fed. She even gave him snacks? He tries to eat dinner, but his wife can see his stomach about to burst through his suspenders.

Harry Brown knows precisely where the man went, and how much he paid, and what the snacks were. Harry and Molly like to share gossip at her showroom, especially at closing time. She knows what men wear under their suits. He knows where they take their suits to be pressed. For both Molly and Harry, it is simply a matter of business as pleasure. They keep tabs on their trade.

So one day, in the late Twenties, before everything went to hell – even before the San Francis Dam burst, driving 180 feet of water from the Grapevine all the way to Ventura by the ocean – Harry looked especially vivid. He had something he could barely keep to himself (and Harry could keep a world war and white slavery to himself).

'You're trying to say then?' Molly coaxes him on.

'That a crime is being built in Los Angeles larger than anything you read in the newspapers.' Then he went on about how much money, how many people.

What on earth could that crime have been? I suddenly wondered if I had slipped into an espionage novel? No matter how often I asked what crime, Molly didn't drop a stitch. Like all the old folks I interview, she was eternally loyal to the memory of dead friends, in this case Harry Brown. 'Go look it up,' she said.

I found circa 1928 letters in what remains of Harry Brown's files. They looked like drivel, about the All Year Round Club, a booster campaign run by the power broker of LA, publisher Harry Chandler. I noticed Harry Brown's name on the roster; and Walt as his secretary. Harry also co-signed a letter from Protestant women's groups railing against bootleggers (at least ten thousand in LA). Another letter, also with his name on the masthead, condemned the movie industry, after scandals involving actor Wallace Reid dying of a drug overdose, comedian Fatty Arbuckle's trials for rape and murder as well as, finally, the unsolved murder of Paramount director William Desmond Taylor.

The mayor's office was being pressured to tighten the screws, morally speaking. That meant, as always, more restrictions against the black community on Central Avenue, especially when by 1924 membership of the Klan reached its highest numbers ever. It also meant tightening the covenants on deeds, to make sure people did not sell to blacks, Jews, or swart types.

Five years later, after Walt was fired for some reason, Harry filed letters on an elaborate plan for a multi-ethnic LA carnival. It would pretend to support 'the amalgamation of all races.' 'Local people (of ability)' would be asked to 'give small displays, distinctive of their particular country. The Japanese, for instance, are exceptional gardeners (something along the lines of the famous Chrysanthemum tableaux of Japan).' The movie industry would be 'asked' to set up a Parade of Nations at various studio locations with 'tableaux' (vivants, no doubt) to help sell real estate in Hollywood.

Was a grand scheme buried in all this ephemera? The police also intercepted letters, which wound up in Harry's files, from Sam Clover, editor of *The Los Angeles Evening News*. Clover lived near Molly, across from Echo Park Lake. Harry used to vilify his name. Clover ran a campaign against the corrupt water policies in LA. But his newspaper went out of business once the damning municipal light and power bonds were passed anyway.

Harry also collected notes passed between Clover and Louis Adamic, the radical social critic who began LA studies in the late Twenties. Clover knew Jake Zeitlin, the muse of the highly marginalized avant-garde in Twenties LA. Zeitlin, in turn, lived near Molly, up in Edendale, at the junction of Alessandro and Alvarado, a block north of where the Sennett studios had just shut down.

Occasionally, I found a letter that sounded more corrosive, like the following by journalist Thelma Nurnburg to her editor/publisher at *The Examiner* in 1928: 'Maybe by the time this letter reaches you, the (Saint Francis) dam business will be all dried up. They ought to settle it by blaming someone. He'll probably deny it, but it will do nicely, editorially speaking.' When this dam burst in 1928, it sent an eighty-feet-high wall of water from the high desert to the ocean thirty miles away, killing nearly four hundred people. The famous water commissioner, William Mulholland, was disgraced after that, and drove himself ('I envy the dead') to an early grave.

I try to concoct a noir murder mystery out of Harry's junk mail. My problem, however, is separating Harry – and Walt – from the movie *Chinatown*. In Robert Towne's script for *Chinatown*, water scandals from 1906 and 1928 were juggled ahistorically into a cinematic 1937. The film is a masterpiece of fiction improving on the truth. Mulwray is obviously Mulholland; the Albacore Club stands in for Chandler and his cronies, who set up water policy, as well as the All Year Club among dozens of other booster boondoggles. Then, to make matters even worse for me, another

290 murder films have been shot no more than five minutes from Molly's house. Every time I outline a treatment, the ghosts of dead screenwriters turn it into a B-movie murder from 1947.

But little by little, the vast crime that Harry Brown mentioned to Molly became very apparent. Harry did not mean a specific scandal, a specific murder, a Julian swindle, or a wall of water. He sucked in his stomach, looked at himself in the mirror. Molly shrugged, as if to say 'Call it your winter storehouse.' Harry was overwrought after an unusually long week listening to twenty versions of false information, all of it linked, but all of it hidden – what added up to a parallel universe. He was talking about the crime of vastness, of an immense pinball machine of greed and misadventure. He was overwhelmed for the moment by how much goes unnoticed that he is required to keep in his file cabinets. He had gotten a particularly sick earful that week. He needed to howl at somebody. The 'boosting of the city,' as he called it (a pun on boosterism), had 'gone epic, even by my standards.' The city had tripled its population in less than fifteen years. One out of five barrels of oil in the entire US came from the new LA fields.

'The crime, then, was this bubble by 1928,' I said to Molly.

'Have you heard the expression fish don't know they're wet?' she answered. I've decided that Walt is a drop in the bucket. The crime was the urban pathology itself, from 1920 to 1986. That would be my story, with Walt's corpse as emblematic of traces we cannot decipher. And Molly as the great sieve of forgetting, the guardian of all that we really don't want to know.

I rummaged for more documents. Molly's friend Dolores, who died eight years ago, has been seen, or at least heard, up in her attic. Apparently, the wild cockatoos up in the date trees are mimicking her sounds. Her ghost stands next to cardboard boxes filled with family photos and portraits. On the second floor, she left an archive of used clothing (1919–78). In life, Dolores used to iron each dress and blouse that she could no longer wear, then stack it face down, like one of Gogol's dead souls. By the time Dolores was sixty, the piles had gathered to the top of her closets. And she lived another eighteen years.

Dolores also packed away letters, in the buffet; along with the French cutlery left by her uncle, the skinny chef from Alsace who had a stroke in 1959 (Molly always found him young for his age). Among Dolores' photographs, I found two of Harry Brown; one in particular, of him standing in a troika with three men whom no-one can remember. They were posing at noon in front of the Eastern Columbia Building, right after it went up (1929). Harry was looking at something off camera. He seemed concerned, as if it would go away, or possibly get in the way. According to Norman Klein in *The History of Forgetting*, Harry believed that every great city has a folklore about its own demise. And in these fables, we find secrets about how it was built, or taken apart. Los Angeles was supposed to be Babylon resisted, the urban chaos stalled in its tracks, quite literally, a garden city that could forget how to age. Harry Brown was behind the scenes for much of that. For him, the entire mechanism of Los Angeles was a crime story, more the whole than any character.

As Harry always said, LA was meant to be a Protestant fantasy of the pleasure dome. He was quick to add that the moment downtown was paved in 1882, they put it under electric arc lights. I would add that in Chinatown and up the Mexican hillside at Chavez Ravine, the roads were never fully paved.

Harry had a theory about LA as Babylon on wheels, first by rail, then by freeway. Like the Spanish *ciudad lineal*, LA was 'a city (...) derived by locomotion.' As a result, neighborhoods could be buried behind this circulation – as the DVD-ROM will show. Indeed, the LA Harry Brown knew even as a boy was already a lineal city (not concentric like Paris or Vienna). It was already growing literally like a vine, from 1885 onward, along trolley lines. It merged city into farm land, with beach-town suburbs past the wilderness. That's what Harry saw as early as the 1890s, before his misadventures in the Philippines (1901).

A lineal city is designed for forgetting, Harry would add. It is not like the concentric city; it does not strangle people into submission. Instead, lineal LA dissolves them into the air. LA forgets by way of evacuation and absence. Even the myths of LA promote this sense of absence, of a city without neighborhoods, without any urban culture. It makes a perfect setting for burying bodies.

Of course, Harry was basically wrong. He spoke for the downtown elite, who had their suits cut at Molly's store. In fact, behind the trolley lines, followed by the lineal freeways (mostly after 1951), LA is very much a city of microclimates, tucked in canyons, in swamp fills, in lake basins; and in traces of farms sold off to make towns. These little townships were then clustered around nodes made by the radial system of roads. LA is nested, but not empty.

Angelino Heights is one microclimate that Molly knew brick by brick. Harry thought he knew the entire city that way. In my next book, I will take us through Harry's Los Angeles (he helped LA oil barons play poker in Veracruz during the Mexican Revolution; and helped more, they say, into the 1970s). For now, Harry is an ornament in Molly's story. He sips dishwater coffee behind her showroom. He talks about his extremely young wife, and shudders. 'All wives get younger over time,' Molly warns him.

Molly knew the immigrant microclimates best, in Echo Park, south of downtown, and east in Boyle Heights. But she serviced the Anglo upper crust. Only once did she actually try out the posh set, in the Franklin Hills, near Chandler's imaginary mansion for *The Big Sleep*, where General Sternwood talks about orchids having the 'flesh of men.' Molly got into trouble up there; and Harry helped her pay the damages. 'Afterward I learned to stay put.'

By 1925, Molly fell in love with Ocean Park, also filled with immigrants, but exotic to her. In the shadow of the thrill rides, she behaved like a dime-store Daisy Miller – the Protestant *converso* let loose. But Molly's version did not contract malaria, never paid the price for her indiscretions ('Why pay for what others get for free?' she liked to say). Molly thought the ocean front walks at Pickering and Lick piers were 'Our Italy,' a phrase she remembered from an old travel book about Southern California.

One day in 1923, she was watching a slapstick movie being shot by the beach while the Lick Pier was burning down. The wind blew funnels of smoke along the shoreline, and out toward the Palisades, luckily beyond camera range.

Zones of Death

In Chandler's *Little Sister*, a screenplay rewritten as a novel, Marlowe notices how effortlessly he becomes a celluloid copy of himself. He 'kills a cigarette,' tries to light another and inhales deeply, 'as though that scrubby little office was hilltop overlooking the bouncing ocean – all tired cliched mannerisms of my trade.' Then, in chapter eighteen, the movie mogul Ballou lectures to Marlowe on how flat and manipulative story writing can get: 'If suspense and menace didn't defeat reason, there would be very little drama.'

We sense Chandler's disgust with LA, with moviemaking, and with his body. He never fully never recovered after meeting the fierce deadline for *The Blue Dahlia*, then checking himself into the hospital. We tend to ignore what that anomie means for many crime writers. Redundancy is a plague for them (consider Doyle's struggle to escape from Holmes). So they write out the agony. Thus, the key to a well-timed murder is not the action, but the deep inhalations, the pauses, absences. The action ceases, and the story is at war with itself. The detective, as writer, is literally lost in regrets.

Molly had a gift for handling that level of regret. She treated it as lost inventory, something for a dollar sale. I profoundly admired her for that, especially when she announced, 'I never dream. And if I do, it goes where it wants, I go where I want.' Sometimes, she was almost transcendental, a Buddha controlling her stomach acids and brain waves. She would fit sliced Wonder Bread inside a wire mesh. Then she would place it on top of a gas burner, next to her percolator. Next, very slowly, she would drift toward the cupboard. While the toast burst into flames, she occasionally would throw me another clue.

She explained that Walt's mother used to play dead for him when he was a teenager. Walt would sit by her bed, in his knickers, pose nostalgically, looking like a magazine cover. Then his mother would pretend to choke, and glaze over. She was devoured by one fear above all – that she would die of a stroke like her mother, at exactly the same age her mother went. So she would rehearse, as if for *Camille*. For his part, Walt had to practice mourning for her. But if the bell rang, she would jump out of bed, and act normal for the neighbors.

Walt's family were, in their way, overly concerned with appearances. Worse still, Walt's father never thought there was anything all that strange going on. He was too busy practising contempt for his son. His father was a martyr to business, and very practical. At their income level, there was simply no money to even think about mental illness.

'You mean Walt faked his own death?' I wondered out loud. Molly was scraping her toast. She was smiling delphically this morning, perhaps trying out a new angle for her smile, something for the customers.

'Death can seem very fake when it happens. I had quite a few customers who claimed they were experts on death. They were mostly fakes.'

'How did you know they were fakes? Not if you see violent death up close.'

Molly nodded, and smiled back. Walt, I guess, was an exception to most rules. He had seen something in the war, but came out mostly confused. In 1945, wood debris from an explosion landed on his head. He was out for ten minutes. When he awoke, he'd been captured by the Germans. After the war, on the first of each month, he received a check from the government for his wartime disability. He also had a nervous tic, every so often made a clicking sound like dentures being readjusted. And he seemed neurotically involved in gadgets, especially portable radios and electric shavers.

Molly let on that she knew something about death. At the age of eleven, she saw a little boy die after slipping off a roof. The ambulance, like a chariot, took the child to the hereafter.

Was Molly confusing this child with Archie, who also fell off a roof? Archie was still alive, drinking himself to death a few blocks away. His stories were even dicier than Molly's. He said that Walt was a disgrace to his gender, but apparently, according to Archie, had a large penis 'that looked just like him.' Not so wonderful, I guess. 'What's more, he was a little swish.' Archie – who had since gone to his middle-name Samuel, or Sammy – started to do a little jitterbug step. Sammy misses the dance halls that used to go all night long back in the Forties, during the swing era. I try to imagine him as a soldier back from the Pacific, trying to grab ass on a crowded dance-floor.

That night, someone tried to break into my house. I had nodded off downstairs, was startled by a tapping against the mullioned window. I jumped out of my skin. The man jumped back, looked frail but big. Then, he foamed over the mullioned window; why, I couldn't imagine. Then I went into a walking coma, grabbed two very dull kitchen knives, and minutes later found myself standing on the porch screaming at him, bluffing about slicing him like a roast, waving my knives. He reacted by throwing a lug wrench at me. Time passed strangely. And that was it.

The next day, Sammy/Archie came to do me a favor. He had found Walt. For only fifty dollars, he'd take me to him. Apparently, Walt had risen from the dead, and was now living in a rooming house off Western. It smelled like cat urine, none of it in Walt's style. A few residents, with embattled faces, had seen Walt just the other day. He apparently looked more lumpen than ever, like a one-celled panda, with black eye sockets. None of the other descriptions matched. One of the old-timers added, 'You know Walt is wanted for murder.'

Speaking about myself, I've seen almost no blood firsthand since I was a child. Back in Coney Island, they would beat each other with chains and bats. I got into a few fourth-grade fights. I saw a neighbor's boy hit by a car, and knocked twenty feet. And over the years, I have watched seven people linger and die from cancer.

That makes a thin soup for writing about murder. But I know the simple tricks for evoking murder. You can learn them from Jack London stories, or the newspapers. First off, never record the sound of the death-blow – only its impact on the body. The victim's shoulders drop suddenly. Life signals indelibly float away.

In 1959, Walt's head fell back, as if he were fighting to remember, while his nerve-endings slowly shut him down. He lay in the corner, ten feet away. Every few minutes, his body shuddered involuntarily. It must have taken almost ten minutes for him to die.

What I know best is imaginary murder. In movies, they are staged in shadows no more than two blocks long. In fact, in Los Angeles, there are actual zones of death, ideal for murdering people in the movies. They are sometimes as carefully marked as hospital parking. The most famous zone is centered in and around downtown, inside a three-mile radius – north into the rail yards, and the river embankments; and west straight into Molly's orbit.

During the noir era, 1944 to 1960, movie murders tended to cluster around the Plaza, and into Olvera Street, then down Broadway, with the ziggurat of city hall presiding somewhere in the background.

Since the Seventies, murders have been relocated a few blocks west, because gunfire looks more ironic underneath the LA skyline at night, seen best from hills in Temple-Beaudry (that were cleared of houses after 1979).

Let us say, the vaults contain one hundred thousand hours of murder filmed inside this zone of death. Its trace memories are ghosts, like Dolores, who finally agreed to stop haunting her attic. Her grand niece couldn't sleep through all the clatter upstairs at night.

But generally these movie locations look very sedate, much too everyday for crime melodramas. That is, until you add oblique camera angles, low key lighting, tracking shots and ominous music to change quiet neighborhoods into troughs of despair. But consider how little outside the frame will make the final cut. I cannot describe the pleasures of excavating what lies around the frame, around these imaginary murders – the humanity that they need to ignore. Molly walks blindly past a thousand of these movie corpses just on the way to work.

So I have made another decision about my story: The journey through the evidence is more exciting than the crime itself. We want to see everything that is erased to make the story legible. We want to visit Balzac at his desk as he gathers his research to begin a novel. Balzac worked so fast, with something like a quill, as if he were engraving the page; so fast that the top of his desk was worn away by the abrasion of his fat forearm, by the sweep as he wrote.

Preparing for a movie murder is more poignant than deciding which one percent survives into the finale. You see past the frame of the picture, get a context. You understand how the story lies. You circulate inside and outside the characters, see who they are modeled on. You find moments for the actors to build character: how people tilted their head in 1937; how men with a big gut stood in 1944; how women positioned their hips; how people avoided each other in crowds; how crowds were different when most people were not there to shop.

You study the dentistry of city streets, dissolve the future into the past. Collective urban memory, like guilt, bleeds through, but elegantly, very tangibly. You can actually control how much paranoia, or eroticism belongs in a scene. At last, you arrive at Harry Brown's state of mind; and the reasons for Molly's gift of erasure.

You see erasure writ large. You study the results of misremembering on the zones of death and on the orbits of Molly's life; and on her sister Nettie's life; Jack's; Walt's; Dolores'. And dozens of other characters who exist a foot out of the frame. You can visit and map the unfindable. All at once, terms like witnesses after the fact, simultaneous distraction, erasure, social imaginary are solid.

And with that, Walt's murder will be simple to explain – as you will see inside the DVD-ROM. It makes the plot points legible, in order to hide vaster crimes, larger paradoxes. We sense these like a stare that is not returned, by their evacuation, by the power in their absence.

Finally, Molly loses her house, and is sent to a convalescent home. There she bloats out like a barge, with nothing to hide or remember, and no-one to care. As she dies, her cancer makes war with her body. At last, only the cancer can be fed. So the nurses decide to starve her to death, to reduce her pain. Molly achieves closure with her step-daughter. They speak quickly about what happened to Walt. 'I loved the way he cut his nails,' Molly says hoarsely. 'He dolled himself up before they took him away.' The nurses give her unlimited morphine while she can swallow a bit, then morphine only on her tongue.

But Molly lingers on. She achieves an eternal instant. People begin talking around her, assuming that she has gone into a coma. In fact, she now can only hear, and think matters over.

Jack appears, her first husband. He understands her better than he ever could in life. Jack looks a bit like Walt suddenly, as if they were genetically merged. There is kindness all around Molly.

Finally, she settles upon seven moments that gather the most moss for her. I have collected these, and structured the first tier of the DVD-

ROM around them. The second tier takes us into the context that goes with each moment, over a sixty-six-year period in Los Angeles: the characters she knew; the events and neighborhoods that might bring her story to life. Finally, the third tier winds up where I am now. The I who guides you is now, of course, myself. I inhabit 1986. You are somewhere further on.

The third tier is a meta-text (not a deconstruction). It is the structure of what cannot be found, what Molly decided to forget, what Molly never noticed, what passed before her but was lost to us. It is proof that no novel or film (documentary or fiction) can capture the fullness of how a city forgets, except by its erasures, its evacuations.

To follow a restriction absolutely is practically a modernist device like abstraction or automatism. Here, the restriction is story itself. We assume, for the sake of argument, that all novels and all films erase vital facts within cities. Then we search for the absences that stories leave out, in order to arrive at a fresh narrative: absence to generate desire.

Not that I don't love to see a suspenseful killing. But I hate watching every character's problems resolved at the same time. I hate the lengths that are needed to make all of it 'legible.' Moments like these in films often send me to the bathroom early. I flinch at cases of mistaken identity. For me they are not suspenseful, only peevish. I resent having the moral weight of the world get lifted during a car chase, even during multiple orgasms; and most of all, during a murder. The ballet of it sometimes works for me: so many pieces tossed in the air, then landing like a jigsaw puzzle. But it is a bit too precious compared to balletic anarchy.

Most of all, I enjoy characters who are still loose cannons, not a resolution in sight. Do you remember a 1933 Warner Brothers' film with James Cagney as a gangster in the chips? He dresses like a million, to the nines, but lives unchecked, still a con man. Suddenly, from out of the Great Depression, a 'forgotten man confronts him. He asks Cagney for nickel, just for a cup of coffee. Cagney smirks, digs into his pocket, and barks, "Here's a dollar. Buy yourself a poi-co-later.'"

I'm chuckling just writing this down. Those are my moments for a good murder. Power and paradox are still unresolved. The good-hearted local shit-heel still owns city hall.

That is why I cannot abandon Molly an hour from her leaving earth. Those were indeed her cherished, assigned seven moments. She delivered each one to me, sculpting with her hands as she spoke. I wrote them down, have them in the DVD-ROM. But I made up that death scene. (Even though I have seen people at the instant of their death, as many of us have. The final un-breath is godlike, sculptural.)

Molly manages to outwit her stepdaughter, and keeps her house for another three years. Then, a week after convincing the ambulance driver that he had the wrong address, she tells me finally, in precise detail, how Walt disappeared. It's not at all what I expected: Walt was much more in the hands of strangers than I had ever imagined. I can see his face, and Molly's surprise, much more clearly now. They were in the factory. The factory was her ethnographic escape: Serbs, Japanese, Mexicans, Filipinos; not as many blacks downtown back then.

In what follows, allow me to deliver these possibilities to you. I am mentally traveling through the photos and the clippings as they bleed through. I have placed over a thousand of them on the floor, like a mosaic. The journey through these could be called a picaresque, or a pilgrim's lack of progress, a bildungsroman in which no one learns enough about anything.

Most of all, it is an aporia brimming with evacuated possibility, even the details inside Molly's house. (We've photographed her interiors, taken an inventory of sixty-six years of a city in a state of forgetting.) Molly was right about Walt, by the way. He did wear clothes as if they were made for another species entirely. I'll explain as we go.

Digital Murder: The Aporia

To achieve aporia, the ancient Greeks learned how to lose track of the road itself, to be baffled, trained themselves to give the wrong answer to the wrong question. Both Plato and Socrates argued that aporia was a distinct pleasure, and a virtue. Obviously, it feels more like an eccentric pleasure, an agonism. Its surprise can blind-side you, literally drop you to your knees. It can break your faith in almost anything. Systems of aporia were brought from Central Asia by the Seljuks, and then refined by the Ottomans, to brainwash boys who were selected to become Janissaries. They knew that aporia arrived in your mind from a place so unfindable that you finally give in to it. You are swept forward as if by a crowd (perhaps the reason why Adorno and Horkheimer identify aporia as the pre-Fascist impulse within the decay of the Enlightenment).

I lose my way inside the arguments that followed, for millennia after the Greeks, from hundreds of philosophers, novelists, theorists. Aporia meant paradox so extreme as to cause a physical ache. During the seventeenth century, Neoplatonists within the Jesuit order saw aporia as a simultaneous journey. You moved toward initiation, yet at the same time never actually began at all. You were inside a puzzle based on rules that seemed to change every ten minutes: furious flight, utter stillness, like a hummingbird.

Molly's effect on me is as aporetic as anyone I know, even more than my own mother, who bored me into amnesia with her stories about foreigners coming to kidnap me on the way to school.

Most of all, Molly's felt her marriages were aporia. She couldn't say if her husbands felt the same way. Jack certainly talked too much, generally about himself, and more when he drank. But Walt mostly scratched his lower stomach in a rather obvious way, to stop from saying anything in public that he might regret. As a result, Walt may have had few regrets, but he was a social disaster.

In medieval history, the greatest aporetics were able to induce forgetting at will. One group in twelfth-century Provence realized that aporia proved that God and the devil were equal partners in the universe: When you remembered, they explained, you became God, but simultaneously, for precisely that reason, you had to forget as well, because you were also Satan.

An earlier sect of Aporisiacs, as they are called, left scrolls not far from the Dead Sea Scrolls back in the first century. However, no-one to this day can make heads or tails out of them. Like Molly, these aporetics from the time of Jesus knew that once you wrecked your memory (aporisiasm), once you literally burnt away synapses (with a pointed stick, in some cases), your pituitary secreted a hormone that brought considerable pleasure. A Roman aporetic (circa 125 AD) compared it to having sex with yourself, while your mind was convinced that your own body was a stranger.

In storytelling, from the novel to cinema to the computer, all forms of absence and evacuation are aporia. In the history of forgetting, of the erasures within cities (especially Los Angeles), aporia enters urban sociology, along with the traces left by social imaginaries, simultaneous distraction and collective memory as a whole.

As in my quixotic interviews with Molly, the history of forgetting is a pleasure based on absence, on anti-tours, on bleedings through. I could go on: The narrative side of aporia has literally kept me up at night, awoken me at three in the morning. For example, tactical computer games like *Doom* are presumably designed to remove aporia, find closure against the anxieties when the labyrinth gets you lost. But I am convinced that these are, in fact, a labyrinth effect, the pleasures of cheating the program, the myth of absolute freedom in a cybernetic world of absolute predestination.

For computer games and other forms of digital story, in other words, aporia is essential, but we must work very hard, like modernists in 1885, to design new forms to keep the aporetic pleasures alive. And these must be a little fast and dirty, very spontaneous, like a sketchpad on DVD-ROM, in order to locate the absences for unreliable narrators, for aporia.

Consider this: the computer is fundamentally an aesthetics of assets (of database, as my friend Lev Manovich explains). Thus, if ever there were an aporetic model of story, it is the digital. However, we must never trust any use of aporia that suggests it is a problem to be solved. That is like saying that unreliable narrators are a problem, rather than the heart of the modern novel. Too often software cleans out aporia as if it were a virus. I sometimes wonder if the algorithm itself tends to make a loop out of an evacuation. Perhaps we have lost the sense of what gives story presence: Absence.

But in certain ways the computer is not appropriate for story. It cannot deliver the third act, the payoff that books can, or movies. Its attention span is different. It is long-winded and at the same time a hyperactive child. With help from writer-director Norman Klein who is all over the DVD-ROM, and with the superlative leadership of the co-directors Rosemary Comella and director Andreas Kratky, I came up with a model that captures the immersive power of a Balzac novel or a stream-of-consciousness journey through a city (Musil, Joyce, Proust, even Melville – the ship as city – and Virginia Woolf).

The structure works like this:

Of course, first, I must tell you that I do not quite exist – that is, in the *a priori* sense. I am contingent, an invention of Norman Klein. He and I mostly coexist on the page, but once you close the book, not much of me will be following you into the DVD-ROM. I am the opening act, so to speak. But I have been doing my homework. I believe I have found a program that allows me to function as a ghost inside the DVD-ROM, like Dolores, who has been something of a god-send. So if while operating the DVD-ROM you sense another presence breathing down your neck, it will most likely be me.

Now for the structure:

As I mentioned earlier, there are three tiers. The first are the seven moments that Molly remembered when she almost died. You will notice a flow of photographs (a *durée*, if you will) from left to right; and a bleeding through, from back to front. Norman will persist in the corner, a few minutes of video for each moment. Then, below the photos streaming and bleeding through, a band of texts crawls with more information.

The sum of these will be a visual, interactive radio program, where you will finally get the last act in which I begin to reveal the unenviable Walt's final days. Of course, it is not me revealing it. Jack left a diary from 1959 to 1961. Molly inherited it, along with Jack's shoes and his suits.

Put it this way: the seven moments are a kind of modern novel on screen with hundreds of photos and Norman as narrator. You might say they are also a docu-fictional movie. But Jack's story is the land of noir. His orbit is closer to the noir movie structure that you know so well, and of which you will find hundreds of examples throughout the DVD-ROM.

The second tier is more like a contextualization. I like to compare it with Henry James' notion of fragrant. What sort of information would you need to know to fill in the absences left by the first tier? After all, only seven moments in sixty-six years? Thus, in Tier 2, you will learn about other characters in Molly's story, like her sister Nettie. You will learn much more about the neighborhoods within Molly's orbit; and within Jack's orbit.

If the first tier is dominated by photographs, the second integrates a great many newspaper clippings, scanned in as they looked in the newspaper morgue. Each tier, then, comments on a specific medium that tries to make the city intelligible as it erases, collectively forgets, survives from day to day. The history of forgetting is a distraction from the basic reality of urban life in Los Angeles, its quotidian power of survival.

The third tier is the aporia of media itself. It is dominated by film and video imagery, by a vast 'ironic index' of what Molly left out, forgot, couldn't see. It samples from the back-story that gets lost when the movie or novel is made legible. Essentially, ninety percent must be erased to make sense. Tier Three (in)completes a 'making of' so vast that there is really no point in boiling it down, like a tomato sauce, into a feature-length film. All the interviews are gesture-driven, anecdotal: the kind of material novelists and screenwriters use, and actors study, in order to enter their characters.

It is an unmaking, an over-making, a bricolage, an aporia of story itself. At the same time, Tier 3 is simply another genre of story. I am quite convinced that the computer and our media economy have shifted the point when stories begin. Now, we actually enter at the moment *before* the movie is actually shot, *before* the novel is actually drafted. We sit by the side of Balzac at his writing table, as he gathers his notes and immerses himself until the novel pours out as if he were living inside five hundred bodies at once. We look at his face as he imagines its entirety. For an instant, he is all story, and all places. In the end, he will make this sensation into a legible novel.

But on the computer, we don't have to make sacrifices on behalf of the legible. We can stay in an immersive world, and play with ten variations of aporia – the aporetic in drama, documentary film, the novel. We become archaeologists of story and city simultaneously. We also run through trace memories of hundreds of murder movies shot in Molly's orbits, in Zones of Death. We become simultaneously the omniscient narrator and the unreliable narrator, as well as urban archaeologists on evacuations in Los Angeles between 1920 and 1986.

After all, aporia is most of all the instrument of memory itself. Its pleasure is a kind of memento mori, the ache of mortality. Thus, I can call the entire project an aporia. It was conceived, designed, completed and published within nine months. It is a product of 2002, just as I am a ghost from 1986.

I hear the echo of the first moment. Sammy has failed to make it home again. He is sleeping on the lawn, in front of the house that Norman Klein used to own. My dog struggles to not launch into a howl, as Sammy goes into a snore that could awaken the ghosts.

The rooflines of Angelino Heights look a bit like Algiers. The streets could pass for the Midwest in 1925. The Hollywood Freeway roars back. I want to keep speaking to you, but my face seems to be disappearing. Wait for me.

2. Montage and Superposition: The Poetics and Politics of Urban Memory in *Bleeding Through: Layers of Los Angeles, 1920-1986*

Jens Martin Gurr

How does one represent, synchronically as well as diachronically, the complexity of Los Angeles, city of Hollywood myths and inner-city decay, of ceaseless self-invention and bulldozed urban renewal, of multi-ethnic pluralism and ethnic ghettos, a city where both the promises and problems of 'America' have crystallised to the present day? For, while the discourses of urban utopia and urban crisis with all their contradictory ideological implications, of course, are as old as the concept of the 'city' itself (cf. Mumford; Gassenmeier; Teske), Los Angeles has always been imagined in particularly polarised ways:

> According to your point of view, Los Angeles is either exhilarating or nihilistic, sun-drenched or smog-enshrouded, a multicultural haven or a segregated ethnic concentration camp – Atlantis or high capitalism – and orchestrating these polarized alternatives is an urban identity thriving precisely on their interchangeability. (Murphet 8)[1]

Los Angeles, of course, has long been a centre of attention for urbanists as well as for scholars of urban planning and of cultural representations of the city. It has been the subject of innumerable studies, the locale for countless novels, documentary films and particularly of count-

---

1   This passage is also cited in Bénézet 56.

less feature films.[2] However, one of the most impressive renderings of the complexities of 20th-century Los Angeles, and surely one of the most ambitious attempts to do justice to these complexities by presenting a wealth of material in a highly self-conscious form of hypertext, is Norman M. Klein's multimedia docu-fiction *Bleeding Through: Layers of Los Angeles 1920–1986*.[3]

Bleeding Through, which combines a 37-page novella with a multimedia documentary DVD[4] on 20th-century Los Angeles, is based on the fictitious story of Molly, who moved to L.A. in 1920 when she was 22 and whose life and times the narrator of the novella attempts to chronicle.[5] The question whether or not she killed her second husband Walt (or had him killed) at some point in 1959 serves as a narrative hook to launch the reader and user of the DVD on a quest through layers of 20th-century Los Angeles. Thus, as the cover blurb of the 2003 edition appropriately notes, *Bleeding Through* is "a loosely constructed documentary underlying a flexible literary journey, it is an urban bricolage held together by the outline of a novel spanning sixty-six years."[6]

I will here argue that *Bleeding Through* makes full use of the opportunities afforded by the digital medium to represent the complexity,

---

2   From among the innumerable studies, cf. for instance Davis; Fulton; Klein 2008; Murphet; Scott/Soja; Soja 1996b, 2000, and 1996a; Ofner/Siefen.

3   With a novella written by Klein and an interactive interface programmed by Rosemary Comella and Andreas Kratky, it was co-produced by The Labyrinth Project at the Annenberg Center for Communication at the University of Southern California and the ZKM – Zentrum für Kunst und Medien – Karlsruhe.

4   References to the novella, where this source is not clear, will be abbreviated BT, references to the DVD will be given by tier and chapter. For a 44-minute film sampling material from the DVD, see https://www.youtube.com/watch?v=dMX5xuuyIDQ.

5   For the connections between Molly's story and the material on the cultural history of L.A., cf. also the additional texts in the original *Bleeding Through* booklet by Klein's collaborators on the project, Shaw 52; Kinder 54f.; Comella 59; and Kratky 60.

6   Klein's collaborator Rosemary Comella calls it "a sort of stream-of-consciousness interactive bricolage-documentary overlaying a fictionalized story based on a real person" (59).

multiplicity and dynamics of the city in a way no other medium could.[7] I will first establish the contexts for an analysis of Klein's multimedia documentary by outlining the key findings of his 1997 monograph *The History of Forgetting: Los Angeles and the Erasure of Memory*, on which *Bleeding Through* is based to a considerable extent. *The History of Forgetting*, however, also provides the context for *Bleeding Through* in another sense: The flaunted self-reflexivity of Klein's distinctly non-academic and often highly literary work and its attempts at creating a non-linear textuality also highlight the problems of representing the complexity of the city in any 'traditional' linear form, whether in print or in a documentary film. These problems of representation demonstrably lead to the non-linear format of multimedia hypertext in *Bleeding Through*. By outlining the relationship between the novella and the documentary and by highlighting some of the features and design principles of the interactive DVD, I will then show how *Bleeding Through* re-presents the complexity of 20th-century Los Angeles by taking us on a revisionist tour of its history since the 1920s and by pointing out the extent to which fictitious urban imaginaries – the innumerable *films noirs*, detective films and thrillers set in L.A. – have shaped perceptions of the city and even the city itself. I will then more explicitly point out the aesthetic and political implications of the multimedia format, of what one might call 'interactive multimedial docu-fiction in hypertext'. Featuring the narrative and aesthetic strategies of hypertext documentaries, *Bleeding Through* can be shown to deploy rhizomatic structures to do justice both to urban structures and to provide a radically subversive, anti-hegemonic view of 20th-century Los Angeles. More generally, it also critically engages with decades of US politics into the the 21st century and thus points forward to Klein's later work.

---

7   Though a digital database narrative like *Bleeding Through* would now, in the year 2022, almost certainly be set up as a website, the fact that it was placed on a DVD in 2003 only matters to my argument insofar as a DVD is essentially 'complete' and cannot be added to, whereas a web-based presentation could potentially be enlarged and built upon, possibly even in a curated form with further materials being supplied by users.

In particular, I propose to read *Bleeding Through* side by side with Walter Benjamin's *Arcades Project*, which has received an astonishing amount of critical attention in urban studies (and elsewhere) in the last 20 years as arguably *the* paradigmatic text on urban modernity. I want to focus on the urban texture of both texts, particularly with regard to how they represent layers of urban memory.

My particular focus in reading *Bleeding Through* and Benjamin side by side will be on Benjamin's notion of "superposition". The underlying view of the city as a palimpsest and the notion of layered spatialized memory this entails, I believe, accord well with the poetics of Modernist urban poetry (I here discuss "superposition" and "palimpsest" together; for a differentiation, cf. Gurr 2021, 84–109).

Finally, I will argue that the emphasis on urban layers and the frequent overlay montage of older and more recent photographs that is one of the most characteristic features of *Bleeding Through* literalises Benjamin's notion of the "interpenetration and superposed transparency" of different temporal layers referred to as "superposition" (546).

Establishing Contexts: The Problems of Representing Urban Complexity in Klein's *History of Forgetting*

Klein's 1997 monograph *The History of Forgetting: Los Angeles and the Erasure of Memory* is itself highly unusual in its mix of genres: Parts I and IV are scholarly studies of 20th-century urban planning in L.A. and of the impact of filmic representations on the urban imaginary of the city; Part II is the imaginative recreation of the perspective on the city of a Vietnamese immigrant in a novella of some 65 pages (2008, 151–215), while Part III is a collection of creatively essayistic "docufables" (217–243).[8]

---

8   In his "Outline" in the "Introduction", Klein sets out his plan for the book as follows: "In the chapters that follow (Part I), I will examine the map of what is left out in downtown Los Angeles, how urban myths (social imaginaries) have been used as public policy. In the second part, I present a docu-novel, (or novella) based on Vietnamese immigrants who live in areas affected by these policies. In the third part, I present docufables from other residents in these commu-

Klein names as one of his key themes "the uneven decay of an Anglo identity in Los Angeles, how the instability of white hegemonic culture leads to bizarre over-reactions in urban planning, in policing, and how these are mystified in mass culture" (2008, 17).

Referring to what is surely the most drastic urban redevelopment project in 20th-century Los Angeles, Klein states that "Bunker Hill [became] the emblem of urban blight in Los Angeles, the primary target for redevelopment downtown from the late twenties on" (2008, 52). The Bunker Hill Urban Renewal Project, begun in the 1950s and extending into the 21st century, brought the virtually total razing of a neighbourhood, the flattening of the hill and the building of the highrise buildings now popularly regarded as constituting "Downtown L.A.". Similarly, Klein comments on the razing of the "old Chinatown, old Mexican Sonora [...] the old Victorian slum district, and other *barrios* west of downtown, [which] were leveled, virtually without a trace" (2008, 97). Commenting on an eerie commonality of all these 20th-century urban renewal projects in L.A., Klein writes:

> [E]xcept for Chinatown, every neighborhood erased by urban planning in and around downtown was Mexican, or was perceived that way (generally, they were mixed, often no more than 30% Mexican). [...] While East L.A. may *today* seem the singular capital of Mexican-American life in the city, the mental map was different in the forties. The heartland of Mexican-American Los Angeles was identified as sprawling west, directly past downtown, from north to south. Bunker Hill was identified as "Mexican" by 1940, like Sonoratown just north of it [...] and particularly Chavez Ravine. (2008, 132f.)[9]

---

nities, particularly about how their memories are affected by public traumas: drive-by shootings, racist neglect, policies toward immigrants, the Uprising of 1992, and so on. And in the final parts, I examine how literature and other media use techniques of the 'unreliable narrator,' and how the corporate uses of 'unreliable' memory are transforming the cultures of Los Angeles" (2008, 17).

9   Klein also refers to the "policy of shutting out downtown to non-whites [...] since the 1920s" (2008, 132).

In *The History of Forgetting* as well as in a number of essays, Klein further shows how the urban imaginary of Los Angeles has been shaped by images of the city in film, from *noir* to *Blade Runner* and beyond, creating "places that never existed but are remembered anyway" (2002, 452), even arguing that the ideology of *noir* and neo-*noir* films, these "delusional journeys into panic and conservative white flight" also help "sell gated communities and 'friendly' surveillance systems" (1998, 89).

More immediately, *Bleeding Through* – though the details do not all fit – is clearly based on one of the short docufables in part III of *The History of Forgetting*: In a mere three pages, "The Unreliable Narrator"[10] (see ch. 5 of the present volume) tells the story of 93-year-old Molly Frankel, who moved to the city in or around 1920, ran a shop for decades and rented out most of her spacious Victorian house in Angelino Heights to a large Mexican family. Towards the end of the text, the experimental and tentative nature of these musings is pointed out by self-reflexively sketching a genealogy in a number of references both to the tradition of the unreliable narrator and to accounts of the constructedness of historiography and memory since the 18th century: "the Münchhausens and Uncle Tobys [...] German and Central European fiction after 1880 [...] the absent presence that in Michelet's words are 'obscure and dubious witnesses' (1847) [...] the broad crisis of representation in cinema" (Klein 2008, 233).

A similar concern with forms of representation is apparent in the chapter entitled "The Most Photographed and Least Remembered City in the World" (247–262) in *The History of Forgetting*. Klein here comments on previous fictional films and documentaries seeking to record the history of ethnic Los Angeles, such as Kent MacKenzie's *The Exiles* (1961) or Duane Kubo's *Raise the Banner* (1980) and the way in which even these well-intentioned films evade the issue of the razing of ethnic neighbourhoods (cf. 2008, 248f.): "The twin beasts that erased much of downtown – racist neglect and ruthless planning – leave only a faint echo in cinema, because generally one will distract the other, or because cinema, by its very apparatus, resembles the tourist imaginary" (2008, 249). Klein here speaks of the "utter instability of cinema as a formal record, and the fact that

---

10   "Unreliable Narrators" is also the title of a chapter in the novella (BT 26–34).

audiences enjoy this paramnesiac sensation, as memory dissolves. [...] The layering of erasures is essential to moving the narrative along, to its simultaneity, its unreal solidity, its anarchic orderliness" (2008, 253).

Anticipating the self-conscious concern with narrative form in *Bleeding Through*, Klein notes in *The History of Forgetting* that when he began to write about the 20th-century transformations of Los Angeles, he "noticed that [his] scholarship was beginning to resemble fiction" and speaks of the "crossed identity" fostered by this type of writing, "[making] the scholar both reader and character within the same text" (2008, 6f.). Even more directly linking the arrangement of a wealth of materials to the writing of fiction, he comments: "In many ways the materials I have assembled look like research gathered by a novelist before the novel is written, before the writer turns the contradictions into a character-driven story" (Klein 2008, 7). In a highly revealing footnote, he further comments on his concern with form:

> I am trying, with as much modesty as possible, to identify a form of literature that is not simply 'hybridized', or 'de-narrated', and certainly not deconstructed – not a blend of others but a structure in itself, a structure that is evolving [...]. By structure, I mean *how to generate alternatives within the text itself, within the style itself.* (Klein 2008, 20, note 10; italics original)[11]

In *The History of Forgetting*, Klein even points forward to *Bleeding Through* by employing – if only half-seriously – the techniques of hypertext. In a short section entitled "Brief Interruption" in the "Introduction", in a reference to theories of memory and forgetting, he states: "The only solu-

---

11   Cf. also Klein 2008, 7: "There are clear signs that both critical theory and cultural studies have generated what amounts to a new category of literature (as yet unnamed). What names there are sound a bit early in the cycle right now, clearly not what this (genre?) might be called ten years from now: docu-novels, "mockumentaries", false autobiographies, public autobiography; "faction"; phonebooks or chatlines as variations of personal essay; public autobiography; "witnessing" [...]; historiographic metafiction. I would rather not add more labels. Instead, I'll stick to the term "history". That is problematic and fictive enough already".

tion for this introduction is a kind of hypertext (click to page 301). For the reader also interested in memory theory [...] I have included an Appendix [...]. Read it now or read it later, whenever is suits you" (Klein 2008, 14).[12] *The History of Forgetting* in its frequently scrupulous and highly self-conscious concern with narrative form thus clearly points forward to *Bleeding Through*.[13]

Bleeding Through: Multimedia Docu-Fiction on the Erasure of Multi-Ethnic Los Angeles

While *The History of Forgetting* addresses more directly the perversions of city planning driven by greed and racism, *Bleeding Through* tackles them more obliquely if more experientially. It does so by juxtaposing two formats: the 'traditional' narrative of Klein's novella on the one hand and a multimedia DVD on the other hand. The documentary is thus held together by the underlying story of Molly and her life in L.A. between 1920 and 1986.

Klein's constantly self-reflexive 37-page novella *Bleeding Through* has a highly self-conscious first-person narrator who tells the story of Molly and – just as centrally – his attempts to reconstruct it:

> I couldn't trust any of her stories. Not that her facts were wrong. Or that she didn't make an effort. [But] she'd fog out dozens of key facts. Whenever I noticed, she would blow me off, smiling, and say, "So I lose

---

12   Elsewhere in the "Introduction", he refers to the effect of his strategies of representation in the book as those of "digital simulations", "special effects, a morphing programme in slo-mo, when the simulation is naked, when the tiger is obviously three frames away from turning human" (16). This morphing of one image into the other by means of match dissolves is precisely one of the most impressive features of *Bleeding Through*.

13   On the other hand, establishing a connection between the contextual material on Molly's story on the DVD and *The History of Forgetting*, the narrator of the novella comments on "numerous characters in the background [of Molly's story] who may show up, but certainly will appear in future volumes of *The History of Forgetting*" (BT 29; cf. also 32).

a few years." [...] But there were seven memories in the years from 1920 to 1986 that were luminously detailed. (10)[14]

It is these seven memories of key stages of Molly's life around which the novella and the DVD are structured, and which serve to explore 66 years of developments in the city. Set largely within the three-mile radius near downtown L.A. in which Molly spent most of her life, the documentary deals with neighbourhoods such as Boyle Heights, Bunker Hill, Chavez Ravine, Chinatown and Echo Park, the disappearance of which was chronicled in *The History of Forgetting*. As the narrator explains here, this area was the site of the most drastic urban renewal projects in the country continuing over decades: "Hundreds of buildings gone: that could just as easily have been caused by carpet bombing, or a volcano erupting in the central business district" (BT 12). The same area around downtown, however, is also the centre of a filmic universe: "Inside those three miles, under the skyline dropped by mistake into downtown ten years ago [in the 1980s], more people have been murdered in classic Hollywood crime films than anywhere else on earth" (BT 12).[15]

---

14   The "preface" on the DVD, readable above a vintage photograph of downtown L.A. with City Hall still by far the tallest building, similarly makes clear the central principle of this "cinematic novel archive" (Klein 2002, 453) and already highlights its major concerns: "An elderly woman living near downtown has lost the ability to distinguish day from night. Rumors suggest that decades ago, she had her second husband murdered. When asked, she indicates, quite cheerfully, that she has decided to forget all that: 'I lose a few years.' Three miles around where she is standing, more people have been 'murdered' in famous crime films than anywhere else in the world. Imaginary murders clog the roof gutters. They hide beneath coats of paint. But in fact, the neighborhoods have seen something quite different than movie murders; a constant adjustment to Latinos, Japanese, Filipinos, Jews, Evangelicals, Chinese. What's more, in the sixties, hundreds of buildings were bulldozed. And yet, pockets remain almost unchanged since 1940".

15   The novella refers to "290 murder films [...] shot no more than five minutes from Molly's house" (BT 31). The narrator later states that "[s]ince the Seventies, murders have been relocated a few blocks west, because gunfire looks more ironic underneath the L.A. skyline at night, seen best from the hills in Temple-Beaudry" (BT 37).

The documentary database includes hundreds of images, maps, newspaper clippings, drawings and sketches, historical film clips and (for copyright reasons[16]) film snippets recognisably re-enacting key scenes of famous L.A. films merely by repeating the camera movements in basically empty streets in the original locations, but without actors.[17] Furthermore, there are numerous interviews with long-term residents, sometimes elaborate captions, as well as narrative commentary by Norman Klein.[18] Klein's video commentary frequently gives clues as to the story behind the disappearance of Molly's husband Walt, which adds a playful dimension of detective game to the navigation experience, because, such is the underlying fiction, the point of navigating *Bleeding Through* in the first place is to act as a detective on the hunt for such clues. However, as the narrator of the novella comments, "[t]he journey through the evidence is more exciting than the crime itself. We want to see everything that is erased to make the story legible" (BT 37). In the novella, the narrator outlines the structure and function of the DVD as follows:

---

16 For this cf. Comella's short essay on the "making of" *Bleeding Through*; cf. especially 58.

17 The re-shot sequences of films such as *Falling Down, Heat, Training Day, Chinatown, The Last Boy Scout, T-Men, Omega Man, DOA, To Live and Die in L.A.* are frequently iconic scenes with the downtown towers looming in the background. In addition, this section also features maps of L.A. pointing out key locations used in these films.

18 The narrator of the novella (whom one is likely to have identified as "Norman Klein") refers to his materials as follows: "I have about a thousand photographs and newspaper articles, over two hundred relevant movies on file, and over twenty interviews, along with hours of interviews with Norman Klein; and hundreds of pages of text" (BT 27; cf. also 33, 38, 42, 43). The narrator comments on the way the documentary is to be perceived: "I turned toward my research on Molly's life, as if I could edit her sensations into a story that was symphonic in some way, or contrapuntal. [...] I could gather data for Molly's story, and embed it like bots under the skin: newspaper clippings, historical photographs, and patches of interviews. Then I could assemble my assets into a vast database, for a search engine that could be selected according to the senses." (BT 11).

The structure works like this: [...] Each tier [of the DVD] comments on a specific medium that tries to make the city intelligible as it erases, collectively forgets, survives from day to day. The history of forgetting is a distraction from the basic reality of urban life in Los Angeles, its quotidian power of survival. (BT 42)

The first "tier" of the documentary DVD, "The Phantom of a Novel: Seven Moments", structured around the seven key moments of Molly's life in L.A. between 1920 and 1986, is dominated by historical photographs of people and places in the neighbourhoods surrounding Bunker Hill. Thumb-nails of these photographs are arranged in random sequence and can be selected by the user; alternatively, the user can go through the photo archive by enlarging each photo to almost the size of the screen and then continuing either with the photograph on the left or on the right. Making full use of the technical possibilities, the sequence of photographs is not fixed but rather randomly brought up from the archive. Additionally, with each phase of Molly's life, there is a short narrative comment by Norman Klein in a window in the corner – a commentary that can be opened and closed by the user. The narrator of the novella describes this first tier as "a visual, interactive radio program [...] a kind of modern novel on a screen with hundreds of photos and Norman as narrator. You might say they are also a docu-fictional movie" (BT 43).

Tier 2, "The Writer's Back Story", which the narrator of the novella describes as "more like a contextualization" (43), is largely made up of newspaper clippings and establishes the context of other people and places more loosely connected to Molly's story. It collects newspaper clippings covering events and developments occurring during Molly's life, with references to the prohibition and illegal distilleries, the ban on interracial marriages in the state of California in a 1932 newspaper clipping, the controversial reception of a 1941 anti-semitic speech by Charles Lindbergh, the deportation of Japanese Americans during World War II, illicit gambling, the McCarthy era with its Red Scare and the building of air-raid shelters – frequently interspersed with innumerable sensationalist clippings reporting murders in Los Angeles. Additionally, explanatory captions beneath newspaper clippings and photographs contextualise developments, with comments, for instance, on the ambivalent views of Chinatown in the 1920s as both "an exotic place in the popular imagination" and a place "considered as an eyesore, as more brown and black races converged at the Plaza" (DVD 2:1).

Tier 3, "Excavation: Digging Behind the Story and its Locale", is described in the novella as "the aporia of media itself" (BT 43). In five sections, it offers a wealth of further material, here arranged thematically rather than chronologically. There is a section entitled "People Molly Never Met But Would Make Good Characters in Her Story", featuring randomly arranged interviews with twelve residents (including Norman Klein) of these neighbourhoods who comment on their experiences within the social and ethnic developments in 20th-century L.A., the 'Zoot Suit Riots', fear of violent police officers, ethnic festivities, Anti-Communist witch-hunts during the McCarthy era, the 1947 murders of Elizabeth Short – the "Black Dahlia" – and of Bugsy Siegel, or the treatment of Japanese Americans during World War II. Largely consisting of film and video sequences, it is a "vast 'ironic index' of what Molly left out, forgot, couldn't see. It samples from the back-story that gets lost when the movie or novel is made legible" (BT 43). It is also described as

> a meta-text (not a deconstruction). It is the structure of what cannot be found, what Molly decided to forget, what Molly never noticed, what passed before her but was lost to us. It is proof that no novel or film (documentary or fiction) can capture the fullness of how a city forgets, except by its erasures. (BT 38f.)

Thus, neither the novella nor the DVD are to be regarded as a higher-level commentary one on the other; they are mutually complementary: Just as the DVD can be seen as a vast exploration of the themes outlined in the novella, the narrative frequently comments on the contents of the DVD: "Next day, I went into a newspaper morgue, looking for articles on Walt's disappearance. Instead, I found fifty ways to kill a man between 1959 and 1961 (along with five suicides). I've scanned all the articles into a database for you" (BT 24).[19] In the novella, the fictional story of Walt's dis-

---

19   A selection is to be found in ch. 7 of the present volume.

appearance is constantly related to current developments chronicled on the DVD, tying the wealth of documentary material back to the underlying quest narrative: "Among police photos, I find what should be Walt's body. [...] Then I discover that on the same day, the downtown editor cancelled photos about racist crimes, particularly the railroading of blacks and Latinos" (BT 25).

With Molly as its protagonist, *Bleeding Through* shifts attention from hegemonic white males and draws attention to the role of minorities in L.A.'s complex history: Molly, "a twenty-something girl from a Jewish home in the Midwest" (DVD 1:1; cf. also BT 13), is herself a new-comer and an outsider when she arrives in the city in 1920. As Bénézet points out, "[t]hrough Molly, Klein articulates a gendered and minority-oriented revision of the city's history" (69).

From the very beginning, both the novella and the DVD characterise Molly's neighbourhood as a multi-ethnic one.[20] Much of the material centres on transformations in 20th-century multi-ethnic L.A., whether in references to "Brooklyn Avenue with its famous mix of Jews and Mexicans, Japanese and other 'swart' young men" (BT 15; cf. also 40) to "restrictions against the black community on Central Avenue, especially when by 1924 membership of the Klan reached its highest number ever" (BT 30), to the tearing down of Chinatown for Union Station (built in 1939), to the history of mixed Japanese and Mexican neighbourhoods, with a Japanese American family man running a Mexican grocery store (cf. DVD 3:1), the 1943 'Zoot Suit Riots', the Watts rebellion, or the turning of Little Tokyo into "Bronzeville" during World War II, when African Americans and Mexicans moved into the area while the Japanese Americans were held in deportation camps away from the West Coast (cf. BT 22).

The drastic changes imposed by radical urban development projects in areas such as Bunker Hill may well be seen as the central theme of the documentary DVD. The section "Collective Dissolve: Bunker Hill", in film sequences from Kent McKenzie's 1956 documentary *Bunker Hill* and *The Exiles* (1961), maps as well as photographs from the 1890s to the

---

20   In his insert narrative accompanying the DVD preface, Klein refers to a family of "Latino's renting downstairs" in Molly's house.

1960s attempts to recreate Bunker Hill before the massive demolition programme that cleared the area for what is now regarded as 'downtown' L.A. A long sequence from McKenzie's *Bunker Hill* refers to the Community Redevelopment Agency's major plan to relocate 8000 residents of the neighbourhood, to demolish all buildings and to sell the land and have modern office and apartment complexes built (cf. DVD 1:6). This chapter of the DVD also displays images from 1959 and 1960 showing the large-scale demolition of Bunker Hill. A sequence from Gene Petersen's 1949 film "... And Ten Thousand More [housing units]" also refers to the problem of 'slums' in L.A. and the need for urban development. This sequence is captioned "The myths of urban blight".[21] Similarly, the photograph of a model "Redevelopment Study for Bunker Hill, March 22, 1960" is captioned "Cooking statistics to justify tearing down Bunker Hill" (DVD 1:6). Indeed, statistics on the housing situation and living conditions in Bunker Hill appear systematically to have been distorted in order to win public support for the demolition of this predominantly Mexican neighbourhood. In the caption underneath a sequence from McKenzie's *The Exiles*, the fact that "this was a brown and black identified downtown center" is explicitly identified as "one of the reasons it was torn down" (DVD 3:3).

In the interview section, residents comment on racial segregation in L.A. Japanese American Bill Shishima recounts his experience of having to leave Los Angeles in May 1942 as an 11-year-old to be interned away from the coast with his family; retired African American fireman Arnett Hartsfield reports coming to Los Angeles in 1929, "when we couldn't even cross Washington Boulevard on Central Avenue [because of segregation]" (DVD 3:1). Finally, Esther Raucher recalls her experience of first coming to downtown as a white child and of staring at African Americans: "As a child [...] I don't think I'd seen a black person [...]. That's how segregated the city was that you would never see a black person" (DVD 3:1). Tying such developments to the underlying story of Molly, a clip from Jeremy Lezin's 1975 documentary *A Sense of Community* with

---

21   On the discourse of crisis and the frequently disastrous consequences of large-scale restructuring plans in L.A., cf. also Soja 1996a.

references to undocumented immigrants working in L.A. is captioned "With each year, Molly felt the massive immigration from Latin America change the rules in her world." (DVD 1:7).

All in all, in keeping with *The History of Forgetting*, *Bleeding Through* thus shows how 20th-century Los Angeles, in the process of becoming increasingly multi-ethnic demographically, continued to erase the visible traces of this diversity in favour of a de-ethnicised 'all-American' look and feel modelled on the needs of a largely white elite and enforced by representing ethnic L.A. along the lines of the paranoid and implicitly racist aesthetic of innumerable *noir* murder films. It remains to be shown that the attempt at an open, non-hierarchical and anti-hegemonic representation of these complexities is closely tied to the non-linear and decentred form of the multimedia hypertext documentary.

Archival Database Fiction and Questions of Form: Nodes, Rhizomes and the Media-Historical Moment of 2003

The experience of navigating *Bleeding Through* is a fundamentally contradictory one: On the one hand, by making sophisticated use of the technological possibilities of the multimedia database, the fast-paced, multi-dimensional, overpowering, non-hierarchical, multi-faceted documentary recreates the urban experience of 20th- or even 21st-century L.A. On the other hand, there is a nostalgic quality to the experience, which partly arises from the use of vintage photographs, film clips and newspaper clippings which appear to work against the grain of the high-tech mode of presentation – in keeping with Klein's views expressed in *The History of Forgetting* on the constant self-reinvention of the city and the concomitant memoricide of previous layers of its history. However, while these aesthetic and experiential implications of the form are worth noting, the more momentous implications of the form are its implicit politics, which elegantly complement the more explicit political commentary also packaged into *Bleeding Through*.

Repeated references to the editorial decisions that went into the compilation of the material, the frequently self-reflexive narrator of the novella as well as the meta-narrative[22] titles of the DVD's three "tiers" – 1: "The Phantom of a Novel: Seven Moments", 2: "The Writer's Back Story", 3: "Excavation: Digging Behind the Story and its Locale" – already point to the fact that this documentary database fiction self-reflexively foregrounds its own narrative constructedness. This is continued throughout the DVD. In between the interviews with eleven other residents of the central L.A. neighbourhoods, Klein in interview clips comments on his thoughts on Molly, on the writing of the novella, as well as on his own first coming to Los Angeles:

> When we began these interviews [...] we were continually locating details that were half remembered, badly remembered or often forgotten and lost and couldn't possibly be known to her. [...] And it seems that we became almost more interested in locating what she couldn't find, what she had to forget, what she couldn't locate. [...] It's such a great pleasure to not be constrained simply by the legibility of the story. [...] The complexity becomes such a great pleasure. It's such a pleasure noticing what she wouldn't have noticed. [...] So in a way the absences become much more present in these interviews than anything else. (DVD 3:1)

Postmodern literary and filmic explorations of the city, it is true, have already dissolved distinctions between genres, between fiction and discursive exploration; they have self-reflexively highlighted the ambiguous role of the writer or film-maker as both observer and participant in urban interactions; they have highlighted the dissolution of traditional views of the city and have frequently attempted to make the city itself legible as a text; they have set out formally to represent the multiplicity, polyphony and fragmentation of the city through multiple, polyphonic and fragmented textuality (for some of these tendencies, cf. Teske). Similarly, in keeping with the views on the narrativity and constructedness of historiography in the work of Hayden White, Michel de Certeau and

---

22   For the concept of metanarrative as distinct from metafiction, cf. Fludernik; Nünning.

others, many documentaries constantly foreground artifice, subjectivity, etc.[23] Furthermore, precisely the fact that the documentary needs to be manipulated by the individual viewer for anything to be visible at all further reminds us of the mediality and the constructedness of what we are witnessing. The medium thus constantly draws attention to itself – in contrast to much traditional documentary film-making which relies on the reality effect of suggesting that what we see is somehow 'evident' and can hardly be questioned. Hence the paradox inherent in much documentary film-making that is meant to be anti-hegemonic, subversive, etc. but through its very narrative form frequently cannot help being suggestive and (since the viewer is essentially passive[24]), imposes a view of the world. *Bleeding Through*, however, in contrast to even the most advanced filmic documentaries, which still inescapably rely on the linearity of film, makes full use of the digital medium to break linearity. Thus, while documentaries, which are originally meant for collective viewing, induce forms of collective medial experience, the effect of *Bleeding Through* specifically relies on a highly individual experience. The constant need to 'do' something in the process of navigating *Bleeding Through* – all clips are very short, hardly anything happens without being triggered by the user, who is essentially assigned the role of a detective in search of the truth – then, not only foregrounds the mediality, narrativity and construction of the material, it also activates the viewer.

---

23 For a discussion of these tendencies in urban documentaries, cf. for instance Aitken; Hohenberger; Nichols.

24 I am aware, of course, that the tradition especially of British cultural studies has long pointed out the viewer's active role in the constitution of meaning of TV, film and other forms of popular culture; for a discussion of the productive role of the viewer, cf. for instance Winter. Nonetheless, the constant need for active manipulation and the flaunted non-linear and hypertextual nature of the programme in contrast to the reception of even the most experimental, fragmentary, 'postmodern' – but ultimately still 'fixed and invariable' documentary film is bound to have consequences for the constitution of meaning.

In keeping with the promise of the medium[25], the non-linear presentation of the material thus precludes closure, stimulates the discovery of knowledge rather than imposing it and thereby fosters learning without being explicitly didactic.

The non-linear structure of *Bleeding Through* and its dual function of both simulating urban textures *and* of empowering viewers, might be characterised in terms of what Christoph Bode has called "future narratives". Bode designates as a "future narrative"[26] any narrative that describes more than one potential continuation in a given situation and thus does not – as most narratives do – present a development as having already happened in the past and as no longer allowing for different outcomes. Rather, "future narratives" in Bode's sense portray the future as being open and subject to intervention. The decision points at which different future developments are possible are referred to as "nodes". In *Bleeding Through*, the numerous points at which users of the DVD have to make decisions about how and where to continue appear to simulate the nodes and decision points in the city. However, while in most of the cases Bode refers to, the future is at least potentially open for the protagonist of a "future narrative", there is no such openness for Molly as the protagonist – her story is clearly represented as having happened in the past. For the user, however, who becomes the protagonist of the quest through the material, the choices that need to be made do suggest an open future.

Moreover, the aesthetic and political implications of the form can fruitfully be accounted for with reference to the concept of rhizomatic structures. As proposed by Deleuze and Guattari (7–13), rhizomes are characterised by the principles of "connectivity", "heterogeneity", "multiplicity", "asignifying rupture", "cartography" and "decalcomania".[27] If,

---

25   Cf. my discussion of the media-historical moment of 2003 and the optimism about the potentials of digital formats in this chapter as well as the discussion in the interview in ch. 9.

26   "Future narrative" is a term coined by literary scholar Christoph Bode (Bode/ Dietrich). The present outline is strongly indebted to the introduction to Bode/ Dietrich.

27   For a discussion of the rhizomatic nature of hypertext along the lines of these characteristics, cf. Burnett.

as Burnett has argued, "[h]ypertext is rhizomorphic in all its characteristics" (28) – and the ingenious digital interface makes full use of the
medium – *Bleeding Through* may be characterised as fully rhizomatic,
with all the non-totalising and anti-hegemonic implications Deleuze
and Guattari famously ascribe to rhizomatic discourses. Thus, the multimedial, multivocal, multi-perspectival, interactive, non-sequential and
highly self-reflexive experience of navigating *Bleeding Through* brings
out "traits that are usually obscured by the enforced linearity of paper
printing" (Burnett 3) and, like hypertext generally, serves to undercut,
liquefy and question established and hegemonic representations with
their frequently unquestioned dichotomies and *"hierarchies violentes"*
(Derrida 56).

As Marsha Kinder argues in her short essay in the original booklet
of *Bleeding Through*, "database narratives [are] interactive structures that
resist narrative closure and expose the dual processes of selection and
combination lying at the root of all stories" (54).[28] *Bleeding Through* is narrative 'enough' so as to create interest and curiosity, but it flaunts its constructedness and constantly requires its users to select from a wealth
of narrative items and, by means of a succession of such choices, con-
sciously to perform themselves the acts of selection and combination
usually hidden behind the surface of conventional narrative. Database
fictions, in flaunting the arbitrariness of such choices and enabling users
to choose differently next time (but never exactly to retrace their steps),

---

28   Bénézet's allegedly original coinage of the term "database narrative" and her
      claim to harmonise what were previously regarded as the incompatible for-
      mats of narrative and of database (cf. 56f.) are hardly as original as she claims
      – she here merely follows Marsha Kinder's essay *"Bleeding Through* Database
      Fiction" which already attempts a synthesis based on her reading of *Bleeding
      Through: Layers of Los Angeles 1920–1986* (cf. especially 54). Curiously, much of
      what Bénézet somewhat pretentiously presents as the results of "[her] analysis"
      (63) is explicitly stated in Klein's text or the accompanying essays or is blatantly
      obvious anyway: "There are many reasons that may have led Klein and his team
      to privilege a recombinant poetics. My analysis suggests that the presentation
      of an openly multifaceted, critical, and self-reflexive creation was one impor-
      tant motivation" (63).

are potentially subversive purely in their form in that they expose as a construction and fabulation what narrative traditionally represents as a given. By making each journey through the material necessarily a different one – and by thus presenting what is merely material for a story as subject to change and human intervention – these narratives also contribute to the activation and mobilisation of the user in ways that even the most advanced self-reflexive fiction – which, apart from some few formal experiments with non-linearity[29], is still subject to the linearity of print – cannot achieve (cf. also Kinder 54).

True to the frequently enthusiastic conceptions of hypertext digital media as an inherently democratic and potentially liberating form current in the early 2000s[30], *Bleeding Through* already by means of its very form serves to deconstruct hegemonic constructions of history by constantly drawing attention to the medial, discursive, constructed nature of such conceptions. As a user, one is never allowed to forget this is a revisionist, anti-hegemonic, at times polemical re-construction of a repressed, alternative Los Angeles.

What makes *Bleeding Through* even more directly political is that it self-reflexively draws attention to the political implications of its narrative procedures and even explicitly links its own constructedness to a history of political fabrications from the Cold War to the Bush administration. In this vein, the narrator of the novella self-consciously comments on his narrative procedures:

> I need a different model for the unreliable narrator as well as for the fragrant noir world, vital though these have been for modern literature, detective stories, cinema suspense; and for lies the State Department delivered on broadcast news during the Cold War. (This is 1986,

---

29   One might here think, for instance, of B.S. Johnson's 1969 *The Unfortunates*; for a discussion cf. Gurr 2017.

30   I am aware that my interpretation of the centrality of the random or stochastic presentation of the material to the overall 'point' of *Bleeding Through* does not accord with Norman Klein's own rather more sceptical views as expressed in parts of ch. 3 of the present volume as well as in the interview (see ch. 9).

remember. You the reader may have more grisly forms of unreliable news to deal with.) (BT 28).

This passage strikes one as curiously multi-layered and proleptic – one is tempted to say prophetic – political commentary: While *explicitly* referring to 1986 and "the Cold War", it clearly seems to suggest the "lies" of another "State Department", namely Secretary of State Colin Powell's infamous UN Security Council speech on February 5, 2003, which occurred during the very final stages of work on *Bleeding Through*. Reread during of after the Trump presidency, however, it appears to suggest the way in which Trump's Secretary of State Mike Pompeo infamously lied in the Trump-Ukraine affair or abused the office to support Trump's lies about the 2020 election.

A similarly self-reflexive passage on the DVD draws attention to the fact that part of the material originally collected for the documentary was destroyed in a computer crash; however, more than merely suggesting the haphazard, selective and necessarily incomplete nature of even the most scrupulously undertaken reconstruction project, this passage again closely associates the contingencies influencing the production of *Bleeding Through* with contemporary political events:

On November 1 [2002], an electric surge boiled two hard drives for *Bleeding Through*. Perhaps the Day of the Dead came by phone, reminding us that all media looks better as a sketch. We lost four programs. [...]

November 9: The drives still smell like burnt upholstery. [...] On TV, we watch George W. Bush take charge of our future. The Pentagon was working on a Stinkpot called Stench Soup, so foul smelling that it could stop a crowd. [...] They are trying to decide if it would make a good "non-lethal" weapon.

The last paragraph [on Bush and the Pentagon's stink bomb] is completely accurate. The rest is what works for you.

March 23, 2003: A last gasp for the project. The troops are less than 100 miles from Bagdad. (Tier 3, "The Lost Section")[31]

---

31   The text is here presented in written form reminiscent of a typed diary entry.

The novella, too, ties events in L.A. back to the grand national questions, turning what seems a novella and documentary on L.A. only into a *pars pro toto* representation of 20th-century America (and by implication even of 21st-century America). For instance, the problems of violence and murder in L.A. are tied to the "longstanding American distrust of urban democracy" (BT 25):

> Many Americans believe, as they did in Jefferson's day, that equality can survive only in a small town. By contrast, fascism flourishes in crowds. [...] I prefer to make Walt's murder a critique of urban capitalism; but then crime becomes a defense of the suburbs. (BT 25)

In his essay "Absences, Scripted Spaces and the Urban Imaginary: Unlikely Models for the City in the Twenty-First Century" (rpt. as ch. 8 of the present volume), written while he was also working on *Bleeding Through*, Klein describes the results of drastic urban renewal projects. After a long section on some of L.A.'s contemporary problems, he explicitly relates contemporary L.A. to the problems of the US and the world at large:

> In short, the global civilisation has begun to settle in. We see its monuments more clearly, its glitter, its brutality. [...] This is a world that has more than lost its way. It is the best and the worst of all possible worlds, dominated by scripted spaces and social imaginaries inside a level of surveillance, top-heavy economic fragility and media feudalism [...]. And yet its possibilities are extraordinary. (451)

Even more explicitly, this 2002 essay links genre-specific urban imaginaries of Los Angeles, ruthless urban planning and reactionary and paranoid US politics in general (especially of the Bush era). Interestingly, it then comments on this conjunction of urban imaginaries of L.A. and grand national themes as being central to *Bleeding Through*, thus suggesting that it should be seen as far more than a multi-media documentary on the changing face of Los Angeles. This passage needs to be quoted at some length:

> During the noir film era, from about 1944 to 1958, the horizontal imaginary city [of Los Angeles] evolves into a complex grammar. [...] This

noir grammar has become the standard way for broadcast media to dis-report the news, to generate a highly conservative, fundamentally reactionary vision of the world that finally covered up key information about the presidential election of 2000, the Enron scandal, the War on Terrorism, the anthrax attacks, Homeland Rule. [...] Of course, noir re-portage has always been a mode of distraction. [But now], that distrac-tion has become national presidential policy, and CNN, Fox, CNBC pol-icy as well [...] So 2002 shows us a noir scenography as our national vi-sion. We have extended this noir staging into national obsession with surveillance as well. [...] I am currently trying to engage these issues in-side a cinematic novel/archive entitled *Bleeding Through: Layers of Los Angeles, 1920–1986*. (2002, 452f.)

However, while *Bleeding Through* thus both seeks to counter the memori-cide induced by urban planning in L.A. *and*, also critically comments on U.S. politics more generally, the question remains to what extent a cul-tural product which so centrally relies on the individual, the solitary user for its experiential form of negotiating central urban issues and which thus inherently forgoes any chance of fostering a sense of community can ever be truly subversive. Although extremely advanced at the time conceptually and in the programming of the interface, in its implied op-timism about the liberating potentials of hypertext, the work in retro-spect seems characteristic of the media-historical moment of its origin in 2002/2003. Klein himself in an essay written in 2007 (rpt. as ch. 3 of the present volume), states that "[f]or media narratives, I have lost my faith in chance techniques, in hypertext, in neo-minimalism, in clicking and clacking to your own adventure ..." (2019, 260f.; open-ended sentence in original).[32] What the digital format allows for in unique ways, however,

---

32   In a laudatory 2003 review of *Bleeding Through*, Helfand (n.p.) insightfully com-mented on the "digital revolution's promise of new literary forms" and the "brief blossom and fade [of the "experiments in online interactive fiction"]" and – speaking of the "many unfulfilled dreams" of the genre, regards *Bleeding Though* as living up to the promises of the form's technological possibilities. For analy-ses of the technological and literary implications of the digital form and their repercussions in literary studies, cf. especially the classic studies by Aarseth;

is the suggestive visualisation of urban layers as implied in the title of *Bleeding Through: Layers of Los Angeles 1920–1986.*

Urban Layers: Memory, Superposition, Archive

These can be conceptualized in the terms familiar from Benjamin's *Arcades Project, Das Passagen-Werk*, which Benjamin worked on between 1927 and his death in 1940, though the first notes and suggestions go back to the early 1920s. This is a vast collection of about 1000 pages of some 3500 quotations and thoughts on the 19th-century arcades in Paris, organised into 36 folders or sections ["Konvolute"] and a number of essays and outlines. The text is quintessentially a work of *fragmentary historiography* (rather than a *fragmentary work of historiography*), proceeding as it does, not discursively, but by means of the suggestive juxtaposition and montage of quotations from over 800 different sources, ranging from police reports to Baudelaire and from snippets of observation to more or less aphoristic remarks on methodology. Perloff appropriately describes Benjamin's technique as an "astonishing piling up of quoted passages" (25) and suggestively states that "the repeated juxtapositions, cuts, links, shifts in register [...] conspire to produce a poetic text. [...] The most sober documentation [of] police edicts regulating prostitution in 1830 [...] is placed side by side with an extract from Baudelaire or Rimbaud." (43). As Benjamin noted himself, "[t]his work has to develop to the highest degree the art of citing without quotation marks. Its theory is intimately related to that of montage" (458; all references are to the 1999 English edition).

In a way remarkably similar to this type of montage, the urban montage in *Bleeding Through* also makes use of various types of distinctly 'urban' text – pub conversations, street scenes, domestic conversations in various social classes, snippets from popular songs, the language of business transaction, etc. This type of urban montage allows both texts to do

Burnett; Ensslin; Gaggi; Hayles; Landow; McGann; or Sloane. Most of these studies date from the early 1990s to the years shortly after 2003. For Norman Klein's rather more skeptical view, see chapters 3 and 9 of this book.

justice to what urban sociologist Gerald D. Suttles has called "the cumulative texture of local urban culture" (283), defining "local urban culture"
as "a vast, heritable genome of physical artifacts, slogans, typifications,
and catch phrases" (284). He speaks of some cities – and Rome, Paris or
London would, of course, be among the 'classic' examples – as places that
"have a lot of such culture" (Suttles 284). Suttles further mentions

> songs that memorialize [...] great streets or side streets, homes once
> occupied by the famous or infamous, a distinctive dialect or vocabu-
> lary, routine festivals or parades [...] dirty lyrics, pejorative nicknames,
> [...] celebrated wastrels, and so on. (284)

In addition to the built environment, then, the layering of *immaterial* urban memory can also be conceptualised as a palimpsest: Thus, particular
neighbourhoods may be characterised by a dense layering of memories,
anecdote, urban legends triggered by established festivities, parades or
specific buildings such as long-existing pubs or restaurants, which may
be associated with legendary local figures formally or informally memo-
rialised in street names, memorial plaques or drinking songs, poems, or
nicknames.

This sequence of examples appears striking in the context of both
Bleeding Through and the *Arcades Project*, which both also use such trivia
to suggest local texture. Interestingly, Suttles argues that these items of
local culture are richly interconnected in the minds of community residents in that they mutually evoke each other. The "mnemonic related-
ness" (Suttles 294) of such items seems strikingly familiar to readers ac-
customed to the textures of both Benjamin's and Klein's urban evoca-
tions.

In his discussion of the *Arcades Project*, Irving Wohlfahrt links Benjamin's practice to contemporary developments in the arts and speaks
of "Benjamin's [...] hypothesis that the montage technique of the avant-
garde points towards the form of presentation necessary today for a material philosophy of history" (266; my translation). In a related vein, Bolle
comments on the "constellation of thousands of building blocks of text
which are used in an attempt to translate the order of the city into the
syntax of a historiographic text" (Bolle 2010, 19; my translation). In our

context of textualising the city, it should be noted that the German title *Passagen-Werk* – in contrast to the English *Arcades Project*, where this connection is lost – by virtue of the ambiguity of '*Passagen*' as both 'arcades' and 'passages (of text)' suggests a convergence of urban and textual structures that is profoundly resonant in Benjamin's *opus magnum* (cf. also Bolle 2010, 19).

In the *Arcades Project*, the complex structure of the urban fabric with its multiple interconnections is represented in a strongly non-linear form, a hypertext *avant la lettre* (cf. Perloff 31–38; Bolle 2010, 22). There are, for instance, multiple cross-references and some 30 different symbols marking thematic clusters *across* the different folders. This system of internal cross-references instead of a linear presentation strongly invites a kind of hypertextual reading following certain threads or thematic strands; Bolle here speaks of a "network-like reading" (Bolle 2010, 25; my translation; cf. also Bolle 2005).

How, in addition to suggesting "the cumulative texture of local urban culture" (Suttles 283) and its memorialisation, do these observations relate to the poetics of urban memory? In the *Arcades Project*, Benjamin develops a notion of the interpenetration of different layers of time and of their simultaneous co-presence in urban space, a phenomenon he refers to as "superposition" (172, 418, 854 *et passim*). This concept is never set out discursively in any coherent way by Benjamin; thus, what Bolle (2000, 413) states about Benjamin's notion of historical cognition, namely that is has to be re-constructed from a large number of fragments scattered throughout the *Arcades* book, is also true of his notion of "superposition" and the reading of the layers of meaning in urban history. Isabel Kranz has here spoken of "Parallelstellenexegese", the need for a synoptic reading of numerous parallel passages (115). My reading of Benjamin's notion of "superposition" is indebted to Dieter Hassenpflug, who has explored its implications for urban semiotics. Hassenpflug summarises the idea as follows:

> [Superposition is] the ability to remember the new – for instance by regarding present urban elements as elements of a spatialised memory and, in so doing, as anticipations of prospective urban realities. [...]

The technique of superposition points to history which is preserved in the elements of cities. (2011, 54)

Given a certain frame of mind – and Benjamin clearly characterises this frame of mind as that of the *flâneur* – this simultaneous co-presence can be perceived and understood by an urban observer. He even speaks of this "interpenetration and superposed transparency" of different times in a given space as the "perception of space [unique to] the flâneur" (Benjamin, 546): "Thanks to this phenomenon, anything that ever potentially happened in a space is perceived simultaneously. Space winks at the flâneur: 'Well, whatever may have happened here?'" (Benjamin, 418; translation modified; cf. also 4, 390, 392, 418, 462, 841, 854, 879f.). Thus, "superposition" refers to both the temporal layering and to the ability to perceive it; Hassenpflug even refers to it as a "technique" (2011, 54).

It is important to note that this type of perception is possible even if the space no longer offers any points, traces or clues to which these layerings can be anchored. Thus, the notion of superposition allows for a *remembered* presence: what matters is what an observer knows, remembers or associates with a site. The following passage from *The Arcades Project* in another characteristically Benjaminian formulation makes clear the role of this knowledge to the perception of urban space:

> That anamnestic intoxication [anamnesis in the medical sense of knowing about a pre-history, the pleasure, the intoxication of having these levels simultaneously present] in which the flâneur goes about the city not only feeds on the sensory data taking shape before his eyes but often possesses itself of abstract knowledge – indeed, of dead facts – as something experienced and lived through. This felt knowledge travels from one person to another, especially by word of mouth. But in the course of the nineteenth century [this refers to the literature on Paris, of course], it was also deposited in an immense literature [...] Wouldn't he, then, have necessarily felt the steep slope behind the church of Notre Dame de Lorette rise all the more insistently under his soles if he realized: here, at one time, after Paris had gotten its first omnibuses, the *cheval de renfort* was harnessed to the coach to reinforce the other two horses. (417)

The past of a site, then, does not necessarily have to be physically seen to be remembered and to inform an observer's perception.[33]

In an excellent discussion of Benjamin's view of modernity in the *Arcades Project*, Brüggemann speaks of two types of modernity, represented by Breton and Le Corbusier, of which the latter conceives of the metropolis as a space of "geometrical order and functional separations [...] absolutistically related to the present", while the former regards it as "a memory and image space of mutually overlaying and interpenetrating periods" (595; my translation).[34] Though he does not comment on Benjamin's concept of "superposition" here, it lies close at hand in the notion of the city as a time-spanning space of layered memory, an understanding which clearly anticipates all the still current notions of the 'city as palimpsest'.[35]

In *Bleeding Through*, the changes in 20th-century Los Angeles are rendered in a fascinating if oblique way in the frequent pairings of an old photograph and a recent one taken from exactly the same angle; some of these are made to blend into one another in fascinating match dissolves or 'bleeds'.[36] Thus, there is a pair of photos taken on the corner of Spring and Main Street in the 1920s and today, in which a shop sign "D.W. Wong Co. Chinese Herbs" disappears and a billboard advertising "Green

33   The discussion of the *Arcades Project* and of superposition as allowing for a "remembered presence" in these paragraphs follows my discussion in Gurr 2021 and 2022.

34   The German original reads: "absolutistisch auf die Gegenwart bezogen [...], ein Wahrnehmungsraum geometrischer Ordnung und funktionaler Trennungen" [Corbusier] vs. "[ein] Gedächtnis- und Bild-Raum einander überlagernder und durchdringender Zeiten und Zeit-Räume" [Breton] (Brüggemann 595).

35   For an excellent recent discussion of the urban palimpsest, cf. Mattheis 49–82; for various aspects of the 'city as palimpsest' notion, cf. Assmann; Butor; Freud 16–18; Gurr 2021, 52–109; Gurr 2022; Harvey 66; Hassenpflug 2006, 2011; Huyssen; Martindale; Mattheis/Gurr; Sharpe/Wallock 9; Suttles. For a theoretical exploration of the palimpsest, cf. Dillon.

36   For the use of such techniques in city films, particularly in Pat O'Neill's L.A. film *Water and Power* (1989), cf. MacDonald 232–234.

River Bourbon" dissolves into a billboard advertising a $ 7,000,000 lottery draw in Spanish (cf. DVD 1:2). In another of these dissolves, juxtaposing 1941 Main Street with a contemporary image, "Fond's Pants Shop" on 655 Main Street (with "Ben's Barber Shop" and "Adams Radios & Appliances" next to it) turns into "Dongyang Machine Co." (cf. DVD 1:3).

Another pair of photographs morphs the area around the South Hill Street funicular "Angels Flight", with buildings around six floors in height, into the present-day high-rise towers of downtown. A further iconic match dissolve overlays a 1943 image of South Main Street with City Hall in the background as clearly the tallest building among a few modest shops in small two-story buildings (cf. fig. 1) with a modern image of City Hall and with the small shops replaced by the glass-and-steel block of the old Caltrans [California Department of Transportation] Annex building (cf. fig. 2).

This is a highly interesting site: Less than three years after the 'new' photo was taken in 2002, the old Caltrans Annex building was torn down to make room for the new HQ of the Los Angeles Police Department completed in 2009 (cf. fig. 4). This, in turn, is directly opposite another landmark building, the spectacular *new* Caltrans District 7 building on 100 South Main Street, completed in 2004, designed by Thom Mayne's Morphosis Architects (cf. fig. 5).

The resulting overlay (cf. fig. 3) was also used as the cover illustration of the 2003 box set.[37]

---

37   For these match dissolves or 'bleeds', cf. also the interview in ch. 9.

Figs. 1 and 2: Juxtaposition of two images of South Main Street with City Hall in the background, one from 1943, one from 2002. Source: 2003 ed. of 'Bleeding Through', booklet, p. 48. The images are also used in a match dissolve on the DVD.

Fig. 3: The resulting montage, presented as a match dissolve on the DVD and used as a cover illustration for the 2003 edition of 'Bleeding Through'.

Fig. 4: LAPD HQ, completed in 2009, now occupying the site of figs. 1–3. https://www.tutorperini.com/projects/justice/lapd-administration-building. Reproduced by permission of Tutor Perini Corp.

Fig. 5: Thom Mayne/Morphosis Architects' celebrated 2004 Caltrans District 7 building directly opposite LAPD HQ. Its building site would have been directly behind the photographer when the photograph in fig. 2 was taken in 2002. Photograph by Patrick Vogel for this book. Used by permission

Given the radical changes in 20th-century Los Angeles, in which older layers of the city where thus frequently "leveled, virtually without a trace" (Klein 2008, 97), this representation of urban layers and their superimposition and interpenetration strongly suggests Benjamin's notion of "superposition", and although he is not explicitly mentioned in *Bleeding Through*, Benjamin is a strong presence in the text (cf. the interview in ch. 9 below).[38]

Thus, if *The History of Forgetting* provided an archaeology of 20th-century L.A. as the *Arcades Project* did for 19th-century Paris, then *Bleeding Through* in its non-linear presentation of a broad range of materials even in terms of form approximates Benjamin's representational strategies in the *Arcades Project*, if in an early 21st-century format. In this vein, the overlay montages or match dissolves as arguably one of the most suggestive features of *Bleeding Through* simulate the "interpenetration and superposed transparency" of different temporal layers that Benjamin refers to as "superposition" (546). The argument both *The History of Forgetting* – explicitly – and *Bleeding Through* – implicitly – make is that even layers that are gone "without a trace" (Klein 2008, 97) matter to the city because they matter to the people who continue to live there and who *do* remember.

This memorial potential of Klein's medial configuration of the city is particularly due to its hypertextual structure. In order to conceptualise

---

38   In its major source, *The History of Forgetting*, however, Benjamin is explicitly referred to several times. The book even includes a six-page speculative piece,
"Noir as the Ruins of the Left" (233–240; rpt. as chapter 6 of the present volume),
in which "Benjamin does not commit suicide; instead, he takes a boat to New
York and winds up among the German emigrés. Being too much of a scholar of
the city streets, he elects not to live in the Pacific Palisades, not to bow at the
feet of Thomas Mann. [...] Benjamin moves instead to Boyle Heights. [...] [He
writes] fifty pages of notes for a Los Angeles *Passagenwerk*, nothing as elaborate as what Benjamin planned to write on the Parisian arcades. (Klein 2008,
233–235 as well as ch. 6 of this volume). Moreover, Benjamin is mentioned in
Klein's 2002 essay "Absences, Scripted Spaces and the Urban Imaginary: Unlikely Models for the City in the 21st Century" (rpt. as ch. 8 of the present volume)
written during work on *Bleeding Through*.

this archival and memorial function of literary and cultural production, one might draw on a conception that shares the media-historical moment of *Bleeding Through*, namely Moritz Baßler's notion of the archive (2003/2005).[39] Baßler defines the archive as follows:

> We will use the term archive to designate [...] the sum of all texts of a culture available for an analysis. In the archive, these texts are accessible without being hierarchized. The archive is a corpus of texts. Within this corpus, passages equivalent to each other can be marked with a search request, as it were. These passages form an intertextual *structure of equivalence.* (196; my translation)

Following George P. Landow's notion of a "convergence of contemporary critical theory and technology" (subtitle), Baßler then suggests that this theory of textuality, of intertextuality and of text-context relations might quite literally be translated into a methodology of contextualising cultural analysis based on data-processing technology (cf. 294). Thus, he refers to the cultural archive in the sense of such a totality of available texts as a "full-text database" (Baßler 293; my translation) accessible by means of search requests and organised in the manner of a hypertext. Indeed, Baßler's entire terminology and methodology suggest a view of the cultural archive as the collection of heterogeneous and not necessarily contemporary texts in a synchronic, non-hierarchically ordered hypertextual database. This 'archive', it is easy to see, will fulfil an important function in maintaining and shaping cultural memory. This notion, tied as it seems to a specific media-historical and technological moment, appears to be literalised in *Bleeding Through*.

All in all, *Bleeding Through* thus functions as a structural and functional model of urban complexity, flaunting the spatial and temporal structures associated with the city in order to represent the non-linearity of urban environments, not least by means of fully hypertextual structures. Most characteristically, *Bleeding Through* uses the digital medium to *literalise* Benjamin's notion of "superposition" in a form of

---

39   This was developed in a postdoctoral project ('*Habilitation*') completed in 2003 and published as a monograph in 2005.

overlay montage or match dissolve to represent the interpenetration of these layers.

Bibliography

Aarseth, Espen J. *Cybertext : Perspectives on Ergodic Literature*. Baltimore, London: Johns Hopkins University Press, 1997.

Aitken, Ian, ed. *Encyclopedia of the Documentary Film*. New York: Routledge, 2005.

Assmann, Aleida. "Geschichte findet Stadt." *Kommunikation – Gedächtnis – Raum: Kulturwissenschaften nach dem 'Spatial Turn.'* Ed. Moritz Csàky, Christoph Leitgeb. Bielefeld: transcript, 2009. 13–27.

Baßler, Moritz. *Die kulturpoetische Funktion und das Archiv: Eine literaturwissenschaftliche Text-Kontext-Theorie*. Tübingen: Francke, 2005.

Bénézet, Delphine. "Recombinant Poetics, Urban *Flânerie*, and Experimentation in the Database Narrative: *Bleeding Through: Layers of Los Angeles 1920–1986*." *Convergence: The International Journal of Research into New Media Technologies* 15.1 (2009): 55–74.

Benjamin, Walter. *Das Passagen-Werk*. Ed. Rolf Tiedemann. Frankfurt/Main: Suhrkamp, 1992. 2 vols.

Benjamin, Walter. *The Arcades Project*. Trans. Howard Eiland, Kevin McLaughlin. Cambridge, Mass.: The Belknap Press of Harvard University Press, 1999.

Bode, Christoph, Rainer Dietrich. *Future Narratives: Theory, Poetics, and Media-Historical Moment*. Berlin, Boston: de Gruyter, 2013.

Bolle, Willi. "Die Metropole als Hypertext: Zur netzhaften Essayistik in Walter Benjamins 'Passagen-Projekt'." *German Politics & Society* 23.1 (2005): 88–101.

Bolle, Willi. "Geschichte." *Benjamins Begriffe*. Ed. Michael Opitz, Erdmut Wizisla. Frankfurt/Main: Suhrkamp, 2000. 2 vols. I, 399–442.

Bolle, Willi. "Metropole & Megastadt: Zur Ordnung des Wissens in Walter Benjamins *Passagen*." *Urbane Beobachtungen: Walter Benjamin und die neuen Städte*. Ed. Ralph Buchenhorst, Miguel Vedda. Bielefeld: transcript, 2010. 17–51.

Bolter, Jay David. *Writing Space: Computers, Hypertext, and the Remediation of Print.* Mahwah, NJ: Lawrence Erlbaum, ²2001.

Bolter, Jay David. *Writing Space: The Computer, Hypertext, and the History of Writing.* Hillsdale: Lawrence Erlbaum, 1991.

Brüggemann, Heinz. "Passagen." *Benjamins Begriffe.* Ed. Michael Opitz, Erdmut Wizisla. Frankfurt/Main: Suhrkamp, 2000. 2 vols. II, 573–618.

Burnett, Kathleen. "Toward a Theory of Hypertextual Design." *Postmodern Culture* 3.2 (1993). https://muse.jhu.edu/article/27387.

Butor, Michel. "Die Stadt als Text." *Perspektiven metropolitaner Kultur.* Ed. Ursula Keller. Frankfurt/Main: Suhrkamp, 2000. 169–178.

Comella, Rosemary. "Simultaneous Distraction: The Making of *Bleeding Through: Layers of Los Angeles 1920–1986.*" Norman M. Klein, Rosemary Comella, Andreas Kratky. *Bleeding Through: Layers of Los Angeles 1920–1986* [DVD and Book]. Karlsruhe: ZKM digital arts edition, 2003. 56–59.

Davis, Mike. *City of Quartz: Excavating the Future in Los Angeles.* Brooklyn, NY: Verso, 2006.

Deleuze, Gilles, Felix Guattari. "Introduction: Rhizome." *A Thousand Plateaus.* Trans. Brian Massumi. London, New York: Continuum, 2004 [¹1987]. Vol. 2 of *Capitalism and Schizophrenia.* 2 vols. 1972–1980. 3–28. [Trans. of *Mille Plateaux.* Paris : Editions de Minuit, 1980].

Derrida, Jacques. *Positions.* Paris : Les Editions de Minuit, 1972.

Dillon, Sarah. *The Palimpsest: Literature, Criticism, Theory.* New York: Continuum, 2007.

Ensslin, Astrid. *Canonising Hypertext: Explorations and Constructions.* London: Continuum, 2007.

Fludernik, Monika. "Metanarrative and Metafictional Commentary." *Poetica* 35 (2003): 1–39.

Freud, Sigmund. *Civilization and Its Discontents.* Trans. Peter Gay. New York: Norton, 1984.

Fulton, William. *The Reluctant Metropolis: The Politics of Urban Growth in Los Angeles.* Baltimore: Johns Hopkins University Press, 2001.

Gaggi, Silvio. *From Text to Hypertext: Decentering the Subject in Fiction, Film, the Visual Arts, and Electronic Media*. Philadelphia: University of Pennsylvania Press, 1997.

Gassenmeier, Michael. *Londondichtung als Politik: Texte und Kontexte der City Poetry von der Restauration bis zum Ende der Walpole-Ära*. Tübingen: Niemeyer, 1989.

Gurr, Jens Martin, Martin Butler. "Against the 'Erasure of Memory' in Los Angeles City Planning: Strategies of Re-Ethnicizing L.A. in Digital Fiction." *Selling EthniCity*. Ed. Olaf Kaltmeier. London: Ashgate, 2011. 145–163.

Gurr, Jens Martin. "B.S. Johnson, *The Unfortunates*." *Handbook of the English Novel of the Twentieth and Twenty-First Centuries: Text and Theory*. Ed. Christoph Reinfandt. Berlin/Boston: de Gruyter, 2017. 323–343.

Gurr, Jens Martin. "Palimpsest." *The Routledge Companion to Literary Urban Studies*. Ed. Lieven Ameel. London/New York: Routledge, 2022. 72–86.

Gurr, Jens Martin. *Charting Literary Urban Studies: Texts as Models of and for the City*. London/New York: Routledge, 2021.

Harvey, David. *The Condition of Postmodernity: An Inquiry into the Origins of Cultural Change*. Oxford: Blackwell, 1989.

Hassenpflug, Dieter. "Once Again: Can Urban Space be Read?" *Reading the City: Developing Urban Hermeneutics/Stadt lesen: Beiträge zu einer urbanen Hermeneutik*. Ed. Dieter Hassenpflug, Nico Giersig, Bernhard Stratmann. Weimar: Verlag der Bauhaus-Universität, 2011. 49–58.

Hassenpflug, Dieter. "Walter Benjamin und die Traumseite der Stadt." Hassenpflug. *Reflexive Urbanistik: Reden und Aufsätze zur europäischen Stadt*. Weimar: Verlag der Bauhaus-Universität, 2006. 7–22.

Hayles, N. Katherine. *Electronic Literature: New Horizons for the Literary*. Notre Dame: University of Notre Dame Press, 2008.

Helfand, Glen. "Read Only Memory: A New Interactive DVD Mines Provocative Layers of Storytelling." *San Francisco Chronicle*, 18 September 2003. https://www.sfgate.com/news/article/Read-Only -Memory-A-new-interactive-DVD-mines -2588147.php.

Hohenberger, Eva, ed. *Bilder des Wirklichen: Texte zur Theorie des Dokumentarfilms*. Berlin: Vorwerk 8, [3]2006.

Huyssen, Andreas. *Present Pasts: Urban Palimpsests and the Politics of Memory.* Palo Alto: Stanford University Press, 2003.

Kinder, Marsha. "Bleeding Through: Database Fiction." Norman M. Klein, Rosemary Comella, Andreas Kratky. *Bleeding Through: Layers of Los Angeles 1920–1986* [DVD and Book]. Karlsruhe: ZKM digital arts edition, 2003. 53–55.

Klein, Norman M. "Absences, Scripted Spaces and the Urban Imaginary: Unlikely Models for the City in the Twenty-First Century." *Die Stadt als Event: Zur Konstruktion Urbaner Erlebnisräume.* Ed. Regina Bittner. Frankfurt/Main: Campus Verlag, 2002. 450–454.

Klein, Norman M. "Bleeding Through." Norman M. Klein, Rosemary Comella, Andreas Kratky. *Bleeding Through: Layers of Los Angeles 1920–1986* [DVD and Book]. Karlsruhe: ZKM digital arts edition, 2003. 7–44.

Klein, Norman M. "Spaces Between: Traveling Through Bleeds, Apertures, and Wormholes Inside the Database Novel" [2007]. *Tales of the Floating Class: Writings 1982–2017: Essays and Fictions on Globalization and Neo-Feudalism.* Los Angeles: Golden Spike Press, 2019. 257–280.

Klein, Norman M. "Staging Murders: The Social Imaginary, Film, and the City." *Wide Angle* 20.3 (1998): 85–96.

Klein, Norman M. *The History of Forgetting: Los Angeles and the Erasure of Memory* [1997]. New York: Verso, 2008.

Klein, Norman M., Rosemary Comella, Andreas Kratky. *Bleeding Through: Layers of Los Angeles 1920–1986* [DVD and Book]. Karlsruhe: ZKM digital arts edition, 2003.

Kranz, Isabel *Raumgewordene Vergangenheit: Walter Benjamins Poetologie der Geschichte.* Munich: Fink, 2011.

Kratky, Andreas. "How to Navigate Forgetting." Norman M. Klein, Rosemary Comella, Andreas Kratky. *Bleeding Through: Layers of Los Angeles 1920–1986* [DVD and Book]. Karlsruhe: ZKM digital arts edition, 2003. 60–61.

Landow, George P. *Hypertext 3.0: Critical Theory and New Media in an Era of Globalization.* [1992]. Baltimore: Johns Hopkins University Press, 2006.

MacDonald, Scott. "Ten+ (Alternative) Films about American Cities." *The ISLE Reader: Ecocriticism, 1993–2003.* Ed. Michael P. Branch, Scott Slovic. Athens, GA: University of Georgia Press, 2003. 217–239.

Martindale, Charles. "Ruins of Rome: T.S. Eliot and the Presence of the Past." *Arion* 3.2-3 (1995): 102–140.

Mattheis, Lena, Jens Martin Gurr. "Superpositions: A Typology of Spatiotemporal Layerings in Buried Cities." *Literary Geographies* 7.1 (2021): 5–22. Special Issue *Buried Cities.*

Mattheis, Lena. *Translocality in Contemporary City Novels.* Cham: Palgrave Macmillan, 2021.

McGann, Jerome. *Radiant Textuality: Literature After the World Wide Web.* New York: Palgrave Macmillan, 2001.

Mumford, Lewis. *The City in History: Its Origins, its Transformations, and its Prospects.* London: Secker & Warburg, 1961.

Murphet, Julian. *Literature and Race in Los Angeles.* Cambridge, New York: Cambridge University Press, 2001.

Nichols, Bill. *Representing Reality: Issues and Concepts in Documentary.* Bloomington: Indiana University Press, 1991.

Nünning, Ansgar. "On Metanarrative: Towards a Definition, a Typology, and an Outline of the Functions of Metanarrative Commentary." *The Dynamics of Narrative Form: Studies in Anglo-American Narratology.* Ed. John Pier. Berlin, New York: de Gruyter 2005. 11–58.

Ofner, Astrid, Claudia Siefen, ed. *Los Angeles: Eine Stadt im Film/A City on Film: Eine Retrospektive der Viennale und des Österreichischen Filmmuseums, 5. Oktober bis 5. November 2008.* Marburg: Schüren, 2008.

Perloff, Marjorie. *Unoriginal Genius: Poetry by Other Means in the New Century.* Chicago: University of Chicago Press, 2010.

Scott, Allen J., Edward W. Soja, eds. *The City, Los Angeles and Urban Theory at the End of the Twentieth Century.* Berkeley: University of California Press, 1997.

Sharpe, William, Leonard Wallock. "From 'Great Town' to 'Nonplace Urban Realm': Reading the Modern City." *Visions of the Modern City: Essays in History, Art, and Literature.* Ed. Sharpe, Wallock. Baltimore: Johns Hopkins University Press, 1987. 1–50.

Shaw, Jeffrey. "The Back Story: Reformulating Narrative Practice." Norman M. Klein, Rosemary Comella, Andreas Kratky. *Bleeding Through: Layers of Los Angeles 1920–1986* [DVD and Book]. Karlsruhe: ZKM digital arts edition, 2003. 52.

Sloane, Sarah. *Digital Fictions: Storytelling in a Material World.* Stamford, CT: Ablex Publishing, 2000.

Soja, Edward W. "Exopolis: The Restructuring of Urban Form". Soja. *Postmetropolis.* Oxford: Blackwell, 2000. 233–263.

Soja, Edward W. "Los Angeles, 1965–1992: From Crisis-Generated Restructuring to Restructuring-Generated Crisis." *The City, Los Angeles and Urban Theory at the End of the Twentieth Century.* Ed. Allen J. Scott, Edward W. Soja. Berkeley: University of California Press, 1996a. 426–462.

Soja, Edward W. *Thirdspace: Journeys to Los Angeles and Other Real-And-Imagined Places.* Oxford: Blackwell, 1996b.

Suttles, Gerald D. "The Cumulative Texture of Local Urban Culture." *American Journal of Sociology* 90.2 (1984): 283–304.

Teske, Doris. *Die Vertextung der Megalopolis: London im Spiel postmoderner Texte.* Trier: WVT, 1999.

Winter, Rainer. *Der produktive Zuschauer. Medienaneignung als kultureller und ästhetischer Prozess.* Munich: Quintessenz, 1995.

Wohlfahrt, Irving. "Die Passagenarbeit." *Benjamin-Handbuch: Leben – Werk – Wirkung.* Ed. Burkhardt Lindner. Stuttgart: Metzler, 2006. 251–274.

3. Spaces Between: Travelling Through Bleeds, Apertures and Wormholes Inside the Database Novel

Norman M. Klein

In 2002[1], in the novella for *Bleeding Through*[2], I wrote:

> We're a civilization of layers. We no longer think in montage and collage; we multi-task in layers more and more. We are more identified with the author than the narrative – just think about watching the director's commentary on a DVD. People are developing the techniques to respond to changing visual codes.[3]

Now, five years later, my response to these changing visual codes has deepened. It has altered how I structure essays, novels – all my writing, particularly my next database novel (due out in Oct., 2007), entitled *The*

---

1   The present essay was first written in July 2007. It has been minimally updated with additional footnotes.

2   *Bleeding Through: Layers of Los Angeles, 1920–86* is an archival database novel (over 1,000 assets) that was first exhibited in 2002, at ZKM (Center for the Arts and Media) in Karlsruhe. It was produced in partnership with ZKM and Labyrinth Projects (at USC). The interface design was co-developed by Rosemary Comella and Andreas Kratky, while Norman Klein wrote the story, and was interviewed in video as the narrator, then wrote an accompanying novella for the exhibition brochure. It was published as a boxed set in 2003 and exhibited at numerous media festivals.

3   This passage did not end up in the final printed version.

Imaginary Twentieth Century.[4] What have these past five years taught me, specifically about data narrative?

The Reader/Viewer

In media (games, interfaces, electronics at home and outside – cell phones), the role of the reader has altered noticeably during this decade. So many new platforms have become comfortable to the public: blogs, wikis, my-spacing, u-tubing, iPods, and this week, iPhones.

After two corrosive generations of digital media altering our lives at home, codes even for what a story contains have noticeably shifted. At the heart of this change is home entertainment replacing what used to be called urban culture. The infrastructure for public culture in cities is vanishing rather quickly, particularly bookstores and live theater. That is simply a fact, not a gloomy prediction.

Museums have finally turned into cultural tourism, an extension of home entertainment. Pedestrian life in cities continues to be increasingly dominated by cultural tourism as well – by what I call scripted spaces (by scripted spaces, I mean staged environments where viewers can navigate through a "story" where they are the central characters. Thus, themed, scripted spaces can be on a city street, or inside a game, or at a casino).

---

4   *The Imaginary Twentieth Century* is an archival media novel of 2,200 images (among other related features). In its earliest form, it was exhibited twice at ZKM, in Karlsruhe, first in October 2007 (soon after this essay was written); then in 2009. Then a number of additional exhibitions generated a second interface, based more on the viewer sorting out piles of cards, for a story that operated in clusters (2,200 images re-edited, with many additions). This version is navigated through comic psycho-geographical, interactive maps. The interface worked as software by 2010, was finally published in 2015 – as an online *wunderroman* (a machine that choreographs an archival tale). Then, to complete the cycle of this machine, in 2016, a print component was added; that is, a second, yet different telling of the novel – in a print book – along with critical and ironic essays in the back. The co-directors throughout this eleven-year odyssey are Norman M. Klein and Margo Bistis.

This reconfiguring of the viewer has massive consequences. It has altered our national politics so thoroughly that our republic has, at last, outgrown the "vision of the Founding Fathers". As I often say, half joking, the Enlightenment (1750–1960) has finally ended – quietly, under the radar, like lost mail.

As I also point out, we have become tourists in our own cities; and through the impact of global entertainment, become tourists in our own bodies as well.[5] We visit ourselves as avatars; we replace notions of the unconscious with good medication. We pharmacologically study our bodies as if they were lopsided chemistry sets with faulty wiring. The era of nano logic means that we are to be steadily invaded in almost microscopic ways (medically, pharmacologically, surgically; and then through branding, theming, etc.). It is hardly a surprise, then, that the viewer is increasingly a central character in media stories (games, immersive special-effects films, themed environments, etc.)

Horizontal Tuning

Remember the horizontal and vertical dials on old televisions? Foreheads would bulge. The Rockies would jitter and shrink. I, for one, did not realize that this was a sign of things to come. As finance capital, those TV analog controls have become infinitely, digitally, more horizontal than ever before; and even more jittery.

In response, our sense of space within narratives (games, films, hyper-text literature) has morphed. We literally morph many spaces into

---

5   See my *Freud in Coney Island*, in which I compare the stillness of US mass culture, in the face of crises since 2000, to medication and a low-grade nervous breakdown. But the high slickness of computer design, Hollywood blockbusters, of cable news talk shows all reinforce this cheerful fatalism, so much like the spirit of the picaresque as a symbolic order about decline as a slide, not a collapse (picaresque decline is experienced as slow but relentless – in class hegemonies that feel themselves slipping away, in prosperity failing across the classes, in armies steadily losing ground; when moral chaos is as normal as a bribe; when rogues take charge badly of a growing disorder).

one – time into space – as if we were copying how the global economy morphs labor markets, national boundaries.

It is the ultimate synchronic mode of spatial design. Paradoxes dissolve under its effect. So when you build a media narrative, paradoxes must be carefully brought back into its navigation, almost like re-introducing an extinct species into a lake.

Clearly, our civilization is a comic tragedy, a mess as contrary as any imaginable. And our republic is fiercely in paradox – under assault, clearly in decline. All this hardly suggests the end of "contradiction," but indeed, this global economy pretends to be too horizontal, too much about consumerism for older forms of the dialectic (Marx for one, Freud for another, balance of powers in our national government for another).

We now imagine applying all this to a database novel. We need media story where the paradoxes are inserted carefully. We cannot return to the media enthusiasms of the 1990s, no more obsession with design, new software, and CG polish, with the avoidance of paradoxes. We need to get truly beyond the nineties media exceptionalism, to generate digital stories that are more uneasy, less about the new "flash," the new gamer tropes.

And that does mean neo-noir. We also must not confuse late cyberpunk with fierce critique. Giddy apocalypses in graphic novels are simply heir to H. Rider Haggard adventures and Verne *voyages extraordinaires.* I sometimes love these overdressed jingoistic fantasies about chauvinist adventurers, though I am more of a noiraholic. As long as there is a corpse in low key lighting, I am hypnotized. Neo-noir space operas and FX adventures have wrapped these codes together; just as late minimalist design has been worked into the design of internet screens. This formalism coming out of neoliberal marketing has entered our poetics as well, complicating (even flattening) how we apply noir fiction, twenties graphic design, or noir cinema from 1925 to 1965. We should give up on CG polish, and not congratulate the Internet for wikis and folksonomy. That is like sponsoring the horizontal economy without allowing for much paradox.

And finally, we should never assume that modernism (1860–1960) solved how best to tell a digital story. That means a "nix" to blind worship of dysnarrative as an end in itself. Finance capital (derivative loans, tax havens) is dysnarrative enough without our help. Most of all, that nix has to include forms that feature the "self-reflexive" viewer, as in plays by Luigi Pirandello or Bertolt Brecht, a John Cage event, or a Surrealist manifestation. No kneejerk retro-modernism (modernists and postmodernists alike were obsessed with powerful contemporaneity as form). For media narratives, I have lost my faith in chance techniques, in hypertext, in neo-minimalism, in clicking and clacking to your own adventure...

The Space Between

But then what is left to work with? A great deal, I believe. To set the mood, I'll begin with three possible backgrounds, then introduce seven tools for media narratives (not games, other modes). Finally, I will conclude with a fragment from an essay on database novels written thirty years from now.

I'll keep the pace brisk, as if we were out of time, but truthfully more because it is still historically very early. Global warming aside, we are in an era that lies "in between," like Europe in the early 1840s, or the US in the late 1930s, or England in 1910. We can smell the gunpowder, but don't quite believe it. And we are certainly tired of old avant-gardist bluster. We should not trust noir cuteness, second-life jingoism, glib fatalism, Manichean abjection. We might easily be entering a golden age, quite by accident; and only culturally. Our political condition remains desperate, comical. However, Italy, Spain, England, France all had their golden ages while their population suffered severe declines. But how do we honestly manage that – in narrative? Between mass marketing and academic oligarchies, where is a truly honest place to start, to tell a story? The subject here is database, interface, digital archive.

The Virtues of Decline

Media culture may not have the patience to take the slow, ungainly steps needed to rediscover what literature and theater once delivered – in print media, for metropolises circa 1900. Yet, the potential emerging out of digital archiving remains vast – for groundbreaking modes of storytelling. To realize that potential, to keep an innocent eye, many established story codes will have to be scrapped (for the most part, as far as digital media story goes). That includes film grammar, the three-act screenplay, the well-made play, melodrama, Joseph Campbell tapes. However, we must construct a history of older forms, invent points of origin.

For example, the US and western Europe today remind me of Spain in the seventeenth century. While the population of Spain dropped by two thirds, extraordinary picaresque[6] novels appeared – very raw. They amounted to the birth of the modern novel in many ways, if you extend their influence into England by 1720. (So much else to add, of course: Spanish theater, the (pre-)existential theater of Calderon; the scripted phantasmagoria of Spanish Baroque painting; as the response in Spain and the Spanish Americas to Baroque architecture from Rome.

But in the bone yard that was the Spanish empire, alternatives emerged. The former Spanish Netherlands flourished, even in the midst of collapse around it (religious wars, etc.). Similarly, in the US today, I

---

6   Picaresque novel: Baroque tale of a rogue, usually told in first person. This very well-known form began in sixteenth-century Spain (Lazarillo de Tormes, 1554, et al). In France, it took on the spirit of more sensual escapade (Lesage; also borrowing from Rabelais). In England, beginning with Defoe, it was redeveloped, by Fielding, Smollett etc. Also eighteenth-century philosophical picaresques, as political allegory: Swift, Voltaire, Johnson. The moralism of the nineteenth-century novel shifted the picaresque toward the *bildungsroman* (Mann, from Goethe). Modernists' fascination with the picaresque turned into structuralist and anti-structuralist episodic literature, and cinema. Consider also the twenties Soviet fascination with Sterne (Shklovsky), the revival of picaresque among modern novelists, and in cinema, as well as its crucial role in Latin-American fiction, from Borges forward.

can see exceptional growth. Consider the bizarre economic bloc where I live: California/Pacific Rim/East Asia/El Norte-America. I can already see Asia literally ending at the San Pedro Harbor in Los Angeles. The blurring of borders from Latin America is so advanced that cities utterly unlike Mexico are evolving in this Latino-identified, emerging LA.

What kind of database novels should respond to this economy – to its widening paradoxes? Advanced suburbanism remakes enclaves within the inner city. Consumerati move into these enclaves, next to paupers from literally another world. The children of immigrants are beginning to restructure the politics and material culture in LA. Eventually, all classes and ethnic groups will become immigrants.

Much of this paradox remains unnoticed in computer-driven story, in gaming, second lives, etc. Most of the contrariness that makes LA remarkable is still hidden – beneath Google Earth. Its human scale, its neighborhoods beyond the fancy shopping are not sexy enough to remember. Only the big-bang version of LA. survives, True Crime rapper video games, and spinouts from Hollywood FX movies.

But in a more casual form, like a novelistic database, the scale can be much more intimate; also, much more detailed. Database novels do not have to blow up the universe to get to act three. They can hover uneasily on a human scale, even look unfinished, like an anthropology, more than interior decorating for the end of the world.

However, unfinished is too often considered a sin. Less "visual excitement" (less metallic, plasmic, or holographic) runs against the grain of media marketing. Too often, digital imaging means high finish. An unearthly shine, like a well-oiled haircut, passes for cheerful, upbeat. But truthfully, how often is high finish just a futile attempt at dignity, a way to sell rather than speak – that big smile during a low-grade nervous breakdown?

Truth is: we fall asleep on our monitors. Many American media artists are utterly "afflicted" by overwork, barely above water. They remain cheerfully haunted. Despite their/our best intentions (myself included), we still may be a culture better at forgetting than responding. And the support system for media experiment – for discovery through unfinish – remains very uneven.

That said, I'll run through my list of tools for database novels:

- New Points of Origin: The Book as Renaissance Computer
- The Aperture
- Bleeds
- The Space Between
- Wormholes
- Streaming or Gliding
- The Picaresque

New Points of Origin:
The Book as Renaissance Computer[7]

Thus, new software is often shiny more than "new." Clearly, some origins for new digital story are five hundred years old. In researching for *The Vatican to Vegas*, I discovered that book design by 1550 was clearly responding to a new software – to perspective. This software helped the commercial classes, military engineering, seafaring, mathematics, very much like the computer today.

By 1550, new designs for the index, appendix, footnotes and afternotes all enabled the book to contain, like a computer today, data essential to the commercial classes, in particular. So I structured my "history of special effects" as if the book itself were a Renaissance computer – or a Baroque computer, circa 1650, or its descendant by 1850.[8]

---

7   The first anthology to directly use the term is Neil Rhodes's *The Renaissance Computer: Knowledge and Technology in the First Age of Print* (2000). I first became obsessed with this parallel when researching the histories of emblem books, of Memory Theaters, cabinets of curiosity. By 1995, when I visited the campus at Microsoft, I found a library of these Baroque books there; and very elaborate interest among Microsoft teams (in the antique book as computer). That probably alerted me most of all.

8   Encyclopedic Enlightenment models of the book evolved by 1850. By that I mean the evolving dictionaries, and industrial manuals of the mid-nine-

Similarly, when I worked on *Bleeding Through* (with Rosemary Comella and Andreas Kratky), it became apparent that novels in the eighteenth century also tended toward data,[9] as did stream-of-consciousness fiction in the early twentieth century.[10]

The Aperture

For the database novel, since it often relies on historic archives, these old forms offer "new" tools. Clearly, the act of reading a novel has always been interactive anyway – mentally interactive, that is. Absences set up within the narrative set the reader to work – "inventing," filling in the blanks. No mode of hypertext can equal the evocative power of the reader mentally filling in the blanks.

---

teenth century, the positivist structuralist model for the scientific book, heir to Diderot's *Encyclopédie*.

9   Eighteenth-Century Fiction: This was very much a model I could share in the design of *Bleeding Through*, as well, since the producer Prof. Marsha Kinder began as an eighteenth-century scholar; and both designers, Andreas Kratky and Rosemary Comella, had strong backgrounds in literature. What particularly fascinates me about the eighteenth-century English novel is its casual, conversational mode of departure: similar to what Barthes meant by "The World as Object" (3–12). A seemingly careless ease of discovery enriches newer forms (the novel), in their earlier stages of development. One can see much the same in Hollywood cinema, from 1921 to 1960, and in practically every world cinema imaginable. That disregard must take hold in the media design of database novels as well. We should all become Henry Fielding and Sterne, learn how to infuse the computer novel with "the gentle art of conversation," with rigor that grows out of careless associative discovery.

10   Stream of consciousness fiction: To what degree is a streaming point of view something else when assets dominate: photos, etc. The archival spirit of Sebald's novels suggests the problem – how the outside and the intimate are an aperture, a streaming of gaps, misremembering, and the ruins of action. Very apt for database fiction.

Folklore is obviously "interactive" in that way, since the characters are structuralist.[11] That is, the characters are cyphers, blanks for the reader to fill in. No wonder that small children expect their fairy tales to be read to them in precisely the same way each time, with the same text exactly. They need familiar absences in order to mentally enter, to use the hollow structured character as a vessel, an avatar.

All media relies on absences to tell story. These absences are the essence of each: Literature is blind; therefore, is visually imagined. Cinema is autistic, sees as a machine, not a character, therefore requires film grammar to heighten the absences. And so on. But in that case, what is absence within the computer? What blindness or deafness can be turned into mental interactive story?

It is impossible for any story to be non-linear. Even graphic animation begins and ends (Oskar Fischinger et al.). Similarly, the computer program is a code so linear, even a straight line is less perfect. Chance techniques are merely wider algorithms. Minimalism is essentially more polish, another feature.

The computer program is an almost cosmological form of cubist collage. So what possible absence can a computer program "honestly" generate, without adding finish, removing paradox, putting more greasy shine in your hair?

For *Bleeding Through*, I decided that holes within the stream of plot points were the easiest tool for absence – not unlike holes in games; also in literary fiction, in music; a figure/ground ambiguity in the plot itself. The non-heroine, Molly, was an old woman who might have murdered her second husband. But that was too many years back. You looked into Molly's face for clues, some twitch at least. Nothing. She behaved with a

---

11   By structuralist interactive folklore, I mean the gaps that have been studied within the structure of myth and folklore, particularly in twenties Soviet structuralist linguistics, and in Lévi-Strauss. Even in the design of dolls taken from fairy tales (i.e. the Big Bad Wolf with Little Red Riding Hood inside his dress – gaps for children to mentally fill in, quite literally). The Transformer, the Barbie outfits ... and hundreds of examples in sim games, to build through inversion.

gentle absence, an absent-mindedness in her manner. No criminal secrets lined her face. No dead husbands rotted in her basement. There
were no transitive clues anywhere, except the viewer filling in the blanks,
building a fictional case, a story.

Thus, to make the absences in the novel stand out, the role of the
viewer was repositioned. The reader is asked to identify as the maker
or the engineer, rather than with character. The planned mental echo,
enough to surprise, enough to immerse, was crucial to a database novel.
Over a thousand images and film assets would stream with absences,
like bubbles in a polymer wrap. Or like a stream-of-consciousness novel
– where action itself is almost deleted by the character's state of mind.
Molly's life was filled with secrets, and simultaneous distractions.[12] She
was a Molly who never bloomed. She hated the creaking of her bed over-
heard in the street. She never lets the viewer listen in.

Most important: this is an authored story, where the viewer is the
maker, not the author. The viewer is invited to guess, through research
provided.

Before long, the viewer also drifts through Molly's streets. The neighbor gradually becomes more interested in just inventing a crime; or being immersed in what crime leaves out. Thus, by the third tier (after the
twelfth chapter), the viewer knows more than Molly, who selectively forgets anyway. But more in what sense? Molly clearly inhabits her own experience.

The viewer now meets characters Molly should have known, but
didn't. We travel thoroughly within a three-mile radius of her house.
We discover that in classic noir films, more people have been murdered
within those three miles than anywhere else in the world. So where do

---

12   "Simultaneous distractions" is a term I use in *The History of Forgetting*. A mental
      image (imago) so fierce that any image resembling it gets distracted. That is,
      even if it stands directly in front of you, it is erased, forgotten. Recent famous
      example: how 9/11 resembled the movie *Independence Day* – at first. Then an in-
      version of imago erased the movie. The gaps of mental imagos can be carefully
      widened or shrank – aperture – in computer storytelling as well.

you put the camera? Molly hated crime stories. Even film and photography partially erase Molly, and her city. The more photographic the image, the more apertures it suggests.

In *Bleeding Through*, the width of the aperture was controlled by key words. The effect may seem random, but actually it was planned. To repeat: In a database novel, apertures must be authored. They might *suggest* chance, but that is purely another fiction inside a fact. Chance is an assigned absence.

Baudelaire was a magnificent guide here. His theory of correspondence proved essential.[13] However, only one aspect of this theory worked best – not the moment in his poem *when* Baudelaire evokes synesthesia[14], but more broadly *how* he achieves this effect. How does he get the reader to smell and hear street noises between the letters and words? He orbits around this question throughout his poetry. Correspondence (not illustration) turns data into sensory fiction. It makes "living pillars ... whisper in confusion."[15]

---

13   Baudelaire's theory of correspondence: Usually associated with his poem "Correspondences", but essential to his theory of modernity as well, of the gap (aperture) between codes of the eternal and of the transient (fashion). Baudelaire left these apertures in his poetry to enhance the feeling of the moment, of its dreamy precision and paradox.

14   Synesthesia became an essential goal in Symbolist art, in Rimbaud, later in Kandinsky; and earlier, in Baudelaire. The key for our purposes here: To erase one sense through another generates a sensory aperture. This thrill is extremely powerful. One can also bring McLuhan (and then French post-structuralist theory) into the discussion, around the trade-off when one medium substitutes for another (the wheel for the road, the telephone for the zone of hearing around you, etc.).

15   On Baudelaire's "pillars whispering in confusion" ("Correspondences", 1857.) Also: How "infinite things sing the ecstasies of the mind and senses" (Baudelaire 1857). In French : "Qui chantent les transports de l'esprit et des sens." The verb "transporter" has the triple nuance: to convey, to transfer, to enrapture. It is a process of correspondence in itself. Baudelaire relentlessly selected verbs with multiple mental action, with seasoning. Or what Henry James mean by fragrant, one of many quotes: "their fragrant faces against one's cheek, everything fell to the ground but their incapacity and their beauty." (*Turn of the Screw*, ch. 8). Or the following from *The Golden Bowl* (II:2): "She should find him walking up

We apply correspondence to a stream of photos. The moments when the photos appear do not precisely match what the video narrator is telling us about Molly (I speak in a video insert while the images stream). The photos do not simply illustrate the city, or her story; they correspond, quite a different matter. Correspondence does not match like a documentary film. It leaves holes. The assets in *Bleeding Through* were carefully mismatched. They left room for mental leaps and sutures.

But the aperture cannot be too wide. If the gap is too wide, no mental leap can bridge it. Apertures should generally avoid purely surrealist automatism, as well as chance techniques – not just a throw of the dice or the I-Ching. They are "figure-grounded" ambiguity for the viewer. They echo (silently) Molly's world in Los Angeles, from 1920 to 1986.

Like keyholes, apertures help us enter downtown, but not as cinema – not movie drama nor documentary – as a third form. This third form evokes story around the unreliability of film. Its aperture plays against mental pictures the viewer already has of Los Angeles (mostly from movies). It is a vivid anti-movie or anti-tour of a city.

Bleeds

The interface is an engine that generates gaps. Its navigation moves these gaps along. But how do these gaps help reveal character, setting, the conclusion? How do they fit well (but feel as uneven as life) in the story?

The width and paradox of the gap are its aperture. These apertures must be vivid enough to feel immersive – more like metonym than metaphor. For the philosopher Roman Jakobson, these apertures operate like a brilliantly engineered language disorder.[16] For an instant, the reader cannot select. Meaning is impaired, like a charming aphasia: the

---

and down the drawing-room in the warm, fragrant air to which the open windows and the abundant flowers contributed; slowly and vaguely moving there and looking very slight and young..." (225).

16   See Roman Jakobson's widely republished "The Metaphoric and Metonymic Poles" ('1956).

visual mind cannot transfer the words back to speech. Momentarily, the hierarchy within language is suppressed. To restore contiguity, the reader substitutes, fills the gap. In a computer interface, the design-gaps force substitutions so vivid that the viewer literally enters the space that moves the story along – not symbolically, but as an act of navigation.

For *Bleeding Through*, the designers Rosemary Comella and Andreas Kratky devoted long weekends in LA to matching old photos to streets today – exactly. The past was black and white. The present was in color. Then, by simply "bleeding" (dissolving) the present slowly through the past, the color erased what was. The gap between color and black and white generated an aperture similar to how memory distracts, or even erases. Thus, Molly's odd memory, the erasure of city (history of forgetting), and the unreliability of the photograph all coexisted in the same space. The interface reinforced a central idea that reappears throughout the novel. It sharpened that idea, gave it spatial simultaneity, through metonymy.

The Space Between

My newest database novel is also centered around a woman's life, but with a very different working principle. Titled *The Imaginary Twentieth Century*, it reveals how the twentieth century was imagined before it took place. In 1901, if legends are to be believed, a young woman named Carrie was seduced by four men, each with their own version of the twentieth century. How they all wound up there (Scheherazade in reverse), and where they went afterward, is the engine. The archive includes 2,200 illustrations, photos, film clips, as well as a stochastic sound engine. In all of these, there are gaps carefully assembled, between imagining the future, confronting the present, and watching the future unfold (first museum interface by Andreas Kratky; other software designers would follow after 2008, for the second interface). The engine is a vast misremembering of the future, like an endless plastic surgery that never quite looks like the original.

The period, 1893–1925 (mostly until 1913), was stricken by a sense of "space between" – neither/nor. The full impact of industrial design came later. The world wars were only imagined. The fears of socialist revolution and feminism had not recharted human history. Even the telephones, the cars, the airplanes, the recorded sound, were all phantoms, compared to what happens after 1915 or so.

The interface, the voice-over audios, the constructing of the spaces between images – all must deliver apertures like spaces between. These had to resemble fin-de-siècle print – its unusual page layouts – but the blanks between pictures are everywhere, as spatial infinity, as abstraction. They were everywhere on the streets as well – ads on the windows, kiosks. Collages were simply an artist's answer: spaces between, time overlapping.

Carrie's story takes seven chapters essentially, in two tiers. Each of her suitors imagined a different future.

A. The first is the moon as Africa (Verne and others as imperialist fabulators).
B. The second was the dense mega-city, the metropolis – how to escape above or below the Crowd.
C. The third was the anarchist rumblings of apocalypse and change – the world war that was coming, the feminist movements, the social revolutions soon to come.
D. The fourth world is about building a body that was rebuilt for the future – a body without fatigue.

Each of the four worlds has a gigantic chapter of its own, in tier three (up to four hundred images apiece).

And finally, in tier four, Carrie sees what the imaginary future may actually look like, in 1924–25. The story ends, then retells itself for generations, in a vast archive assembled by the secretary of Carrie's uncle.

Each character, each technological point of view, each city in the story/archive must jibe somehow, add to the comic tragedy. Each must reveal its distortions of the future. In our story, the new century is both a ghost and a noisy, crowded machine. It is industrial vision in a world dominated still by agriculture (the pastoral machine). It is industrial archaeology, industrial photography – in Chicago, New York, Paris, London, Berlin, Berne, Greek hill towns, Los Angeles.

This is fundamentally a novel about seduction – sexual, futuristic, apocalyptic, utopian. The promises never quite add up. It is like plastic surgery failing to look like the original, no matter how many operations it takes. This imagined century delivers other than what it promises. It even delivers Carrie's legend, known finally even to Duchamp. He dedicates *The Bride Stripped Bare by Her Bachelors, Even*, his *Large Glass* to Carrie's legend. That legend becomes another space between in her life.

Even data fields are spaces between. They cannot generate conclusions and second acts in the same way as a novel or a film. Nor should they. So, the apertures become essential, to allow the view to mentally set the speed, determine the rhythm, enter the shocks.

Wormholes

The wormhole is a theoretical shortcut inside an interface. We know about wormholes among stars. Wormhole physics, like computer graphics, is a visualized subjunctive geometry. It is a map of phenomena that seem unfindable, except mathematically, except as echo.

The computer cannot help but evolve wormholes. Its theoretical space always becomes a topos, or a chronotope, or a topology. Simply put, that spiraling milky way of visual data becomes a sleight of hand, a brilliant architecture. Part of this effect is design. The computer program turns mathematical code into user-friendly visual icons and navigation. The wormhole is another space between, quite suitable to science fiction, time travel, being trapped in the wrong body, misremembering the future. The space between imaginary, geometric worlds, and action itself. Shall we ride the circle, or cross the isthmus of the wheel.

Each one of the suitor's worlds has its wormhole effects, ways to transverse, or simply dissolve, into a labyrinth no wider than you prefer.

Computer wormholes are another aphasic visual effect, another metonymic trick upon the eye. Their gaps are so slim, they are endless (but never infinite). The geometry of a program allows you to imagine the four worlds, spaced between gaps set up by the narrator. You can reverse these gaps like a sock, turn Africa into the moon, flip the skyscraper upside down, become the body without fatigue.

Streaming or Gliding: The Animation of the Interface

In *Bleeding Through*, the images stream from left to right. In *The Imaginary Twentieth Century*, they glide, rather than stream, because the complexity of nineteenth-century illustrations was much more architectonic, had to be seen at once, for the mental gaps to emerge. Sliding resembles a stream of consciousness novel. Molly is a Molly Who Never Blooms. Gliding suits a more episodic mode of storytelling. The viewer can move in up to four directions, or seem to.

The viewer animates the archive in order to locate apertures that express the paradoxes, the contrary facts that are also fictions, the spaces between.

The Picaresque

This Baroque mode of storytelling relies on episodic breaks, relatively flat eccentric characters, and the wandering through the labyrinth of the world. Inside this world, space and time misbehave, as if you were inside the daydream of a careless god. You witness the decline of the future, along with its greatest promise. You are an epic failure, in a world of utopian misunderstanding.

I am quite convinced that the picaresque is an ideal form inside a database novel. Thus, by way of picaresque, I can invoke Cervantes, Grimmelshausen, Fielding, Twain, Potocki, Pynchon, hundreds of graphic novels, video games, Philip K. Dick and science fiction of alternative worlds. The picaresque story is often driven by a hidden archive, secret knowledge, a trace memory that never quite answers its questions. It is an oracle with a touch of senility.

The viewer navigates through these archives like an erroring knight more than knight errant. The wormholes, the spaces between, the misre-memberings, the magic that is mostly legend, all conspire, but with very little purpose. The guidance mechanism broke last winter. But something is still running, like a waiter at a bombed-out restaurant.

The picaresque lost its appeal in the mid-nineteenth century. Only in the past fifty years, from Latin-American magic realism to Pynchon to science fiction, has it achieved a comeback, of sorts.

Most of all, the picaresque is a pilgrimage through decline. Americans are particularly fascinated by picaresque now, because it fits into folklore as special effects, escapes into one volcano or another. Americans want to learn more clearly where their decline will lead. They want to see their alienation humanized as a dark joke.

Thus, *The Imaginary Twentieth Century* is a picaresque, perhaps as Duchamp, Twain, Musil, Wilde, Bierce, Woolf and Kafka might have assembled it, might have assembled its aperture. On their behalf, and for all the picaresque that these relentless databases may bring, I offer these two experimental novels, one on stream of consciousness, the other as a picaresque. I manage better when the subject is about loss, selective memory gaps. I am convinced that the computer is a broken necklace that continues to metastasize. It strangles us with user-friendly data. Unless we humanize its savage, comic aspects, our stories will remain as thin as bumper stickers.

For the as-yet-unknown master novelist reading this, I offer my unrestricted support. That is the purpose of this essay, to leave an aperture where newly engaged work can follow.

Bibliography

Barthes, Roland. "The World as Object". *Critical Essays*. Trans. Richard Howard. Evanston: Northwestern University Press, 1972. 3–12.

James, Henry. *The Golden Bowl*. *Novels 1903–1911* [*The Ambassadors* / *The Golden Bowl* / *The Outcry*]. Ed Ross Posnock. New York: Library of America, 2011.

Klein, Norman M. "Bleeding Through." Norman M. Klein, Rosemary Comella, Andreas Kratky. *Bleeding Through: Layers of Los Angeles 1920–1986* [DVD and Book]. Karlsruhe: ZKM digital arts edition, 2003. 7–44.

Klein, Norman M. *Freud in Coney Island and Other Tales*. Los Angeles: Seismicity/Otis Press, 2006.

Klein, Norman M. *The History of Forgetting: The Erasure of Memory in Los Angeles*. London/New York: Verso, 1997.

Klein, Norman M., Margo Bistis. *The Imaginary Twentieth Century*. Karlsruhe, ZKM, 2016.

Rhodes, Neil, ed. *The Renaissance Computer: Knowledge and Technology in the First Age of Print*. London: Routledge, 2000.

4. Los Angeles since the End of Molly's Story: 1986-2021

Norman M. Klein

It has been almost forty years since the closing moments of *Bleeding Through*. Today, our sense of drift is as subjunctive and unreliable as Molly's. Something vast has overwhelmed the American psyche, and is radiating down to Los Angeles. Between 2020 and 2021, the surges of COVID-19 intensified this emerging panic, and Trump's suicidal presence never seems to evaporate. He is obviously a caricature of something much larger: an unending constitutional crisis. Big Lies and blackshirt vigilantism are normal election strategies today. The public looks mostly traumatized, unable to move. Nevertheless, one matter is broadly agreed upon: these 2020 balkanized problems go back forty years. This is particularly apparent in Los Angeles. Since the eighties, Southern California's image of itself has vastly changed. Instead of an erector set of freeways, it is now an archipelago. Photo spreads feature tiny recovered neighborhoods, hidden canyons, lost stream beds, and isolated ecosystems.

From downtown to Venice Beach, food-truck cantinas have popped up – guerilla *loncheras* served by Asians and Latinx side by side.[1] All

---

1   In the sixties, food trucks evolved from the hashhouses and taco stands in LA. that accompanied the waves of Mexican and Asian immigration, often sharing the same neighborhoods. This caught on as a trend nationwide. Some trucks were even rated by Zagat, and their cooks opened trendy indoor restaurants during the nineties. The craze shifted toward fusion, like Korean-Mexican Kogi BBQ, by after 2008, then, after 2018, began again. For this, see Trinh; Gold; Resnick.

at once, a filigree of micro-ecologies replaced the city of circulation. *Loncheras* are a glorified part of the vendor economy, very immigrant-based, "bohemian" (a nineteenth century term for urban transients), but not simply about immigrants. They suggest the medieval caravan, a zocalo on Sunday, a farmer's market, a flea market. It's a long category nowadays. We can add online startups, *elote* street-cart vendors (see Bhimji)[2], home-office handymen, day-labor construction crews, popup vintage clothing stores, itinerant auto repair shops, under-the-table carpenters who convert garages into apartments, Lyft drivers, any temp worker who never gets regularized, even adjunct professors.

Short-term contract jobs are replacing more stable permanent work. Instant startups and peripatetic food trucks indicate how fiercely labor conditions have already changed – not only in the growing service industry, but in manufacturing and construction as well; there is also a steep drop in work for college teachers (see Kezar et al.), and for "creative freelancers" (see Puko). Food trucks (some with Zagat ratings) are the cuter, aestheticized version. But job precarity is more than just urban picturesque. It resembles an economic nervous breakdown, fiercely highlighted by shutdowns during the pandemic. And while the job picture improved slightly by the summer of 2021, there remains a labor crisis that will only grow. Perhaps the Biden Administration rescue plan can slow that down.

Back in the nineties, I called this more varied, more subaltern LA the New Byzantium. I was referring mostly to colossal waves of immigration, starting in 1965. The Immigration and Nationality Act, passed only months after the Watts Rebellion, removed immigration quotas, and helped start a land rush. Within forty years, five million immigrants settled into Southern California. Los Angeles had more foreign-born residents than New York and had become the most ethnographically diverse city in North America (Waldinger/Bozorgmehr 13f.).

That was the setting I lived in while shaping my social imaginary Los Angeles, the unreliable narrators, the layers of the city, and finally,

2   The harassment of Mexican immigrant women vendors by the LAPD finally became citywide news in the summer of 1993 (see Lopez 1993, 1994).

Bleeding Through (see Sanchez). I could barely find schools to educate my son. In LA, a crackup in public education followed the passage of Prop. 13 (1978), and coincided with the growing hegemony, at least for a time, of the San Fernando Valley. Too often, the public sector was treated like a casino investment that didn't pay off. In fact, one of the early names for this withering syndrome was "Casino Capitalism" (Strange 38, 52–55).

Throughout Southern California, many towns suffered vast losses in manufacturing, from auto and steel to St. Regis Paper Company, National Lead foundry, Chevron Chemical Refinery. "Deindustrialization" and "automation" became slug lines for a "two-tier" economy. Plant closures hit South Central especially hard, one of the root causes of the 1992 insurrection.

Offsetting these crippling losses was a neo-mercantilist trade boom with Asia. This was part of a worldwide scramble after the end of Western colonization, and America's inability to continue it. As colonies gained their independence, the US and its NATO allies invaded their economies instead through the World Bank, and multinational corporations. Only through deregulation and hyper-fast banking could this fragile setup continue.

But in the US, that "postcolonial" gambit backfired. It sparked a phenomenon that essentially colonized the United States itself. The US underdeveloped its own infrastructure. Los Angeles could not get its subway and trolley system "untracked" for decades. The mythical California bullet train has languished for thirty years. LA was confronting postcolonial mercantilism, the hallmark of the Reagan/Thatcher era. We must remember that both Republicans and Democrats wanted deregulation. For LA, however, it manifested as a shrinking public sector that reinforced inequality and police abuse. A lot of this was through ordinances. New restrictions against busing flared up in the San Fernando Valley. A zoning and parking lockdown in Hollywood claimed it was just getting the sex industry off its streets. In LA, the politics of real estate highjacked an international neoliberal agenda. Year by year, parking instructions on upscale side streets grew more incoherent and arcane. They helped to create urban satraps from Hollywood to Santa Monica.

The urban core was being colonized as well, from hipster enclaves to increasingly poor, racially mixed slums in South Los Angeles. The towns of Commerce, Bell, Vernon, Compton and South Gate were rocked by corruption, and swept toward bankruptcy. Real estate oligarchies were sanctioned across the LA Basin. This is connected to worldwide mercantilism. Asian capital adored Los Angeles, at first in the beach towns, then in old Protestant enclaves like San Marino. But the coup de grace came after 2009, in the platinum finesse of the arts district downtown. LA was like a reprise of the seventeenth century, of foreign concessions granted to the Dutch and British East India companies along the coastal littoral of India and China. A special-effects cosmopolitanism took hold in LA, similar to New York, London, the Emirates, Luxembourg, the Hong Kong airport. The age of anchor babies and helicopter children had arrived. With neo-mercantilism, instant money is more valuable than productivity. Biden's infrastructure bills might reverse that for a year or two, but consider how deep the problem goes.

Legacy manufacturing (heavy industry) severely declined by the eighties. Factory workers in LA were savagely displaced, almost singled out. In 1971, Chrysler closed its key assembly plant in the City of Commerce. Chrysler, along with GM and Ford, was trying to out-Japan Japan, and failed. As early as 1971, foreign cars already accounted for 41% of sales in LA (the highest percentage in the US at the time) (see Baker).[3] That misery index worsened year by year. LA's eclipse was right in sync with steel and aluminum closures in Youngstown, Ohio, after 1977, marking the birth of the Rust Belt.

By 1985, the problem had metastasized further. That was when Molly finally gave up her tiny garment factory on Main Street, now the capital of homelessness in Southern California. The shop had to be locked tight all day. The general area was dotted with grimy sweatshops that kept chains at the front door to slow down immigration inspectors. The deepest recession in decades overtook most of downtown. Back east,

---

3   "Developers built almost enough new space – about 8 million square feet between 1988 and 1992 – to fill Century City." (Baker). Bob Baker was an *LA Times* Labor Writer (a category that seems to have disappeared nationally).

heavy manufacturing was almost treated as a lost cause. So much had been offshored, so many union jobs transferred to the American south, or lost when big plants over-automated. For LA manufacturing, there had been an ace card. As late as the eighties, aerospace was still grow-ing, but less surely. It had once been concentrated in a belt of 800,000 people from Hughes Aircraft below West LA to the San Fernando Valley. During the World War, it was centered around the Lockheed factory in Glendale/Burbank. By 1945, two thirds of all airplane manufacturing came out of LA county. That was when Victorian homes two blocks from Molly's house were converted into rooming houses. By 1947, Southern California was suddenly the largest industrial hub in the US. The Korean War added even more – exotic missile and electronics contracts (see Scott). Aerospace grew even further when America went into space; and when space travel was computerized with satellites during the Vietnam War. Then came B2 and Stealth bomber research ($500 million to $1 billion for each plan). LA represented a supply chain from Saigon to Berlin. That would transmogrify into a supply chain for goods more than weapons, but not yet.

Missile contracts began to slow down in the eighties, when aerospace actually lost another 18,000 jobs (very uncharacteristic). Then the bottom dropped out: in 1991 Northrop and Lockheed, along with their subcon-tractors, removed over 21,000 jobs (see Vartabedian).[4] Every month, the hole deepened, to about 300,000 overall. Production of B2s dropped by ninety percent.

The University of California lost government grants that incubated tens of thousands white collar technical jobs, especially in engineering. In the crime melodrama *Falling Down* (1993, director Joel Schumacher), the protagonist is a psychotically unemployed aerospace engineer named DFens. He still wears a plastic pen insert in his shirt pocket. Then, in the midst of freeway traffic, he freaks out, and goes on a killing spree. From an army-navy store (in Silver Lake on Sunset), he kills a fascist Cold War salesman, then symbolically carries around a duffle bag filled with anti-tank missiles and automatic weapons. Everything about

---

4   The closures around aerospace continued into 1997.

DFens is a leftover from the Cold War; with echoes added to the 1992 insurrection. If the movie were remade now, DFens might be a software psychotic who joins QAnon.

Ford had already shut down in Pico Rivera (1980), GM in South Gate (1986: my wife taught ESL in Southgate at the time, and the shockwave was apparent in store closures and street turmoil). Firestone closed its famous plant in South Gate (1980, dating from 1927). Goodyear's even more famous plant complex (1920–79) was a chief employer on Central Avenue, in the heart of African-American LA. Tremors were felt across the region. Mike Davis writes about Kaiser Steel's polluted odyssey in southern California, before abandoning Fontana (1982). Overall, a hundred-mile supply chain around automobiles shrank precipitously, from dealerships to auto supply outlets, to trucking.

American capitalism was undergoing savage post-hegemonic redesign. The implications were right on the surface, but often went strangely unnoticed. For example, in 2010, I visited the last fishing boat docked on Terminal Island. The local Japanese fishermen were gone (see Macias Jr.),[5] along with their combined fleet of 250 vessels. Sunkist Cannery had been closed since 1985. At one time, LA produced half of all canned tuna in the US. Now, mackerel replaced tuna as the main LA catch, strictly for the Asian market (see Waters).[6]

I was surprised by the ocean blasts of extreme afternoon heat. A middle-aged sailor was mending a net that symbolically had seen better

---

5   A memorial site was set up in 2002, by the children of former residents who were interned in 1942. One descendant explained: "If something like that happened again, I would be taken [...] Bulldozing this life, this entire community in a non-negotiable way, it's scary. It cannot be undone." (see Macias Jr.).

6   The canneries died from 1918, included Chicken of the Sea (closed in 2001)) and Starkist. The canneries built a company town of 300 houses, for a community of fishermen that ranged between two and three thousand, most of them Japanese. There was still beach alongside the cement. A writer columnist for the *LA Times* wrote: "As the sun rises higher and higher, the smell of fish becomes almost a tangible cloud" (Meares). The entire community was given two days to move, by presidential order. A plaque honoring their ordeal was installed in 2002.

days. There was no one else in sight. The sailor shook his head, explained that he needed to quit. The sadness of this fadeout was overwhelming him. Five hundred feet away, cranes like giant stick insects were unloading hundreds of container ships. Each ship could hold a thousand times what small fishermen like him might catch over an entire year. The freeze trawlers hauling fish were big, but just stegosaurs. Everything seemed to be overwhelmed by the cranes (not unlike those huge conveyors that used to dominate coal mines). Machines of this kind are the folklore of an age. Our urban folklore is cybernetic, a Marvel Universe, less about skylines, and more about AI things against the sky. Our urban gigantism is now quasi alive, but alien.

LA's shipping container industry first replaced small fishing boats during the Vietnam War. Then, the very same shipping routes that serviced the weapons (from Okinawa to Vietnam) were retrofitted to deliver imports back to the US. That is essentially how Japanese subcompacts first arrived in Long Beach (especially after 1970). Southern California's twin ports were tailor-made for container ships. The harbor depth had been originally dredged out of mudflats (by 1913). That was its edge back then over San Diego. These mudflats proved easy to trench ever deeper, once container ships mushroomed in size, to eventually hold 12,000 containers apiece, each container 40 feet long, holding about 125,000 pounds. In 2000, nine million containers (measured as TEU) passed through the ports each year. By 2020, despite the Great Recession, that figure had nearly doubled. The ports had survived more competition, a slump in 2005, five or ten percent decline in certain years – even before the pandemic. However, business was platforming. Essentially, the first wave of globalization was already slowing down, even before the tremors of 2020. Despite these risks, by the Fall, container deliveries to the ports recovered from massive drops to their highest levels ever. By the summer, volume was on its way to a record ten million container units over the year. Experts pointed out that global supply chains were growing treacherously long. Suddenly, the world stood still; but no one should have been surprised. Why was there no default to allow for such interruptions? There is an implacable congestion. A new business model is coming. And it is already showing up in the LA region. Let me explain:

Due to the ports, the nineties LA economy saved itself. The boom in techware would never have been enough. After the Cold War ended, LA transformed into the Eastern capital of the Pacific (the "gateway"). That reengineered life on the ground for a million people at least, across five counties.

The new rules were a "neo-mercantilism." A quick historical note on that term: In the seventeenth century, the Dutch and British East India (joint-stock) Companies were given charters to function as independent sovereigns on behalf of the king. They directly owned their own fleets across Asia. The king did not control their capitalist ambitions. Mercantilism was a pluralist, deregulated form of sheer greed. After 1980, it came back. Inside the kleptocracies of the fading Cold War, multinational corporations were granted unregulated authority over Pacific trade. In the Pacific, Los Angeles was the freebooting major port of call.

After the Gulf War (1991), Pacific trade exploded, led increasingly by China. To keep up, the harbor of Los Angeles made special arrangements with East Asian traders – and particularly with Denmark's Maersk shipping, the largest carrier in the world. By 2005, if you walked across the two ports that constitute the LA harbor, almost no ship docking still flew American colors. At first, these flags represented a partnership, because American multinationals ran the table on globalization in the late sixties. But soon enough, the multinationals themselves became increasingly non-American, set up headquarters in tax-free zones. And their East Asian and West European partners were more than thoroughly independent.

The prologue to this deregulated free-for-all was fifties consumerism, also pioneered in Southern California – bringing McDonalds, Disneyland and cable TV to America. The evisceration (privatizing) of public life began under the banner of consumer fun. Hollywood was already neo-mercantilist in the fifties, through international distribution deals. Most of all, the hegemony of the screen replaced city life. From Nintendo to color TV, the true coming out was the Mackintosh in 1984 (see Levy; Webster). The Mackintosh was announced in a TV ad where the past was blown up as if it were a Hollywood trailer. How splendid and horrible the future has been. We have cheerfully gone along, allowed for new kinds of distortion in our memory, public archiving and even intimacy itself. This economy of the senses is a hallmark of California mercantilism.

The result has been a plastic surgery of the present, without much of a past, or much of a future. Along with medication, this frozen smile was then engineered into themed streets from Horton Plaza to Citywalk, and finally, the Arts District of Los Angeles (see Regardie).[7] But there are signs of downtown glitter hitting a wall after the pandemic. So underneath the hype, the first age of globalization is ending. What does that mean? It is not simply about recession or panic. Global *consumerati* are still around. And yet, something within global trade is crumbling.

The economics of the developed world cannot support the oligarchic side of globalization much longer. The European Union and the Biden Administration have agreed to forbid corporate income taxes below fifteen percent. This is supposed to reign in multinationals, and reduce havens for piracy. Global supply chains cannot meet the climate crisis either. Nation states are reigning in global policy everywhere.

But we are so far along. Heavy manufacturing has long since given way to a service-oriented economy. There is a vast supply chain of industrial parks along our freeway systems. Cold War manufacturing no longer dominates the suburbs. Forgotten inner cities throughout the Basin are starting to "gentrify" (I find that term incredibly reductive).

---

7   Since 2000, "spectacular growth… (boosted) downtown's residential population from about 18,000 to 85,000." (Regardie). Also 500,000 now work downtown, or use downtown (from nearby areas). All of that was frozen during the pandemic. The November 2020 Downtown Los Angeles Community Plan Update projected another 150,000 residents added to downtown by 2040. But these magic statistics sometimes involve magical thinking as well. The pandemic has clearly stifled the future growth of downtown for a few years. The future of many districts in the city depends on five vectors at least: the shrinking of globalization supply chains; the crises in Hollywood (exhibitors especially, like Pacific Arclight going bankrupt in April 2021); the changing logistics from the ports; the future of Silicon Beach. There will be a relative boom, but booms are always selective as well.

But 'Gateway Cities' like Bell and Southgate continue to absorb more immigrants than they could sustain. Everywhere, we find orphans to neo-mercantilism. A new hardening of oligarchy has remade what we mean by segregation, but not removed it.

The Ramparts police scandal of 1997 was shocking, eventually tainted over 3,000 cases, led to investigations or arrests of 2,500 officers (see Weinstein). The Ramparts CRASH anti-gang unit (sometimes called The LA Confidential story in real time) remains officially the "most corrupt" in LAPD history; and that's saying something. The story broke when its kingpin, Raphael Perez turned state's evidence in 1999. His girlfriend admitted to witnessing him killing two men. Officers in Perez's unit had "planted evidence, beaten suspects and covered up unjustified shootings" (Glover/Lait). They were also implicated in a robbery of a Bank of America branch (1997), had falsely detained street gang members, beaten up innocent detainees, and stole huge amounts of cocaine (see Rampart Area Corruption Incident). To the present day, "the ghosts of Rampart hover over" new cases of police abuse (see "Editorial: Ghosts of Rampart").[8]

In the nineties, I lived in the Rampart police district when it happened, had no clue to be honest. Still, I would hear surreal drivel from some police officers arriving from the Ramparts station. One cop refused to bother with fingerprints, asked me why I lived in a slum altogether. Another warned me that my house was the center of an Angel Dust mafia. Those non sequiturs disappeared with more community policing. However, in public hearings and through lawsuits, many residents now complained about county sheriffs behaving badly in the outlying districts of the county.

During the Iraq War, through the 1033 Program, the Department of Defense could "transfer excess military equipment to local law enforcement" (see Lee).[9] Over $7.4 billion in equipment were donated to hun-

---

8   Presumably body-worn cameras can prevent Ramparts-scale abuses in the future. This appeared less than four months before the killing of George Floyd.
9   This scandal was reported throughout the national media after the Floyd murder.

dreds of police forces, including the LAPD – a new boondoggle for defense contractors (see Lee). This weaponizing of local cops, as if they were an army of occupation in Baghdad, was probably more extreme in other cities. But the impact of immigration and growing density[10] and growing inequality could not be ignored here either.

Let us take the long view again: In sync with the growing anti-government mentality of Washington politics, Los Angeles entered a cycle of underdevelopment that one usually associates with the Developing World. Eventually, about one third of all imports into the US arrived through the LA harbors, but only 3 percent were inspected, so the tax revenues are dubious. Was this Pinochet's Chile? Nevertheless, the roar of capital seemed worth cheering about. Those trillions of dollars required a bigger distribution chain within Southern California. What used to be seen as "corridor cities" isolated within the county, along freeways from the ports, were national arteries that would have been impossible in 1960. The delivery of all this merchandise finally stretched a thousand miles or more. The Inland Empire was a key hinge to an expanding nationwide chain of distribution.[11] More trains from the

---

10   Arguments about how to densify Los Angeles, and where to densify, have come and gone over the past fifty years (but have mostly not amounted to very significant changes in the ratio of single-family homes to rentals): see Chiland; General Plan Framework, chapter 4 (on how the number of rentals did not keep up with population growth from 1980 to 1990). Today, one out of three renters in LA spends more than half their income on rent (see Cowan/Gebeloff). This problem was long foreseen. However, the 1970 Centers Concept Plan – arguing for densification of rental housing – had almost no impact by 2007, and only minimally since. It was almost impossible to shift from R1 homes to a rental-first strategy (see Peralta).

11   De Lara traces the Inland Empire's rise underneath the canopy of expanding trade through the ports. Also, there are signs of a 2020 boom in new business construction in Rancho Cucamonga, and other depot sites in the Inland Empire—even during the pandemic. As global supply chains presumably tighten after 2020, the globalized Inland Empire will double more as a revitalized network for American-made inventories as well (cf. CBRE). CBRE is a leading corporate real estate company.

Alameda Corridor[12] continue straight to Chicago[13], or by trucks into Mexico. Transport from the ports is radiating more widely each year. A shift in capital – both eastward and across northern Mexico – is deeply underway.[14]

This new supply chain is a kind of sovereignty outside the United States as well. It also pushes the nation's western boundary into the Pacific as never before.[15] Using seventeenth-century mercantilist imagery,

---

12   See Alameda Corridor Transportation Authority; Zamicho. See also Alameda Corridor Project; Barden. For the enormous growth midway through the recovery from 2008, after the Inland Empire was among the hardest hit in California by the Great Recession, see Kirham: "Overall, the Inland Empire accounted for two-thirds of the new businesses created statewide from 2012 to 2013... Over the last year, Inland Empire jobs have increased 2.7%, a faster rate than any part of California except the Bay Area. That's more than double the rate of Los Angeles County and nearly triple the pace of Orange County. Thursday's report predicts the Inland Empire will add jobs at an even faster clip – about 3.4% annually – over the next five years."

13   "Walmart's warehouse in Elwood, Illinois, operated by 3PL (third-party logistics subcontractor) Schneider, is a block away... where the containers are first opened after having been closed at the factory in China"—transported from the LA ports. There was a strike at this Illinois warehouse in November, 2012. In Los Angeles, seventy workers from ILWU 663 – Pier 400 at the Port of Los Angeles – also struck in sympathy, indicating two-thousand-mile echoes made by this Pacific distribution chain (see Global Supply Chains Research Group).

14   The American artist most involved in recording this maritime transition into Los Angeles, from 1972 onward, was probably Allan Sekula. One of many articles covering his work is Roberts, who argues that Sekula's *Fish Story 1989–95* "expresses a shift from a culture of postmodernism to one of globalism and reflects the artist's effort to renew realist art in the wake of the postmodern culture of the 1980s." Also, Sekula's films *The Lottery of the Sea* (2006) and *The Forgotten Space* (2010). Coming out of a family linked to industrial labor in Erie, Pennsylvania, he grew up near the port of San Pedro.

15   See Port of Los Angeles annual reports, 2006 forward; Port of Los Angeles Facts and Figures, 2000 forward; for the growth of Pacific trade since the 1960's, but especially after 2000, see Sharpsteen; Flanigan; White; Gottlieb. During the pandemic, the ports suffered a decline, but recovered briskly over the late summer, 2020, indicating renewed momentum, even expansion in the future. An incentive program to speed up truck turns, in order to handle the

LA was like a freeport on the Open Sea (*Mare Liberum*),[16] as they called the Pacific in the seventeenth century. Losing aerospace turned LA into a sovereign city state, like Venice in the fifteenth century, or Singapore today. During the nineties recession, LA was forced to self-isolate (see

---

"clogged gateway" was set up in February, 2021 ($7.5 million in incentive rewards; see Mongelluzzo. This came in response to renewed fears of another logistics "meltdown" at the ports, with container ship waits at crisis levels already (Mongelluzzo). All this was a sign of a boom confronting uneven planning and infrastructure (see Tirschwell). The congestion was expected to clear up by late spring "seeing glimpses of improved productivity" (Johnson). Clearly, the post-pandemic trade patterns were somehow different than earlier, not simply a return to anxious normal. I would suggest that new logistics were forced by the pandemic, and that these changes suggest a more permanent shift – differences in the Pacific supply chain, a new era about to begin; probably more about shift in consumer tastes, and certain areas of manufacturing growing, with different needs, a new stage in globalization. Another shift will certainly be toward more infrastructure to support data capitalism at the ports: "Initiatives aimed at turning container ports from conduits of physical freight activity into hubs for the digital information surrounding those cargo movements are underway in virtually every major global gateway." (Johnson).

16 Mare Liberum, or The Open Sea, was a concept developed by the Dutch jurist Hugo Grotius, beginning in 1607. But it was also reframed in defense of the nation state – and strangely enough, also in defense of destroying the nation. Upon the Open Sea – the Pacific today (and the wide open internet) – non-national carriers hemorrhage the American state. They are updates of pirates and privateers – or joint stock companies who were legally vassals of the king, but saw vassalage more as a license to steal (circa 1600–1780). The most exalted of these thieves were the Dutch East India Company, and the British East India Company. Many historians consider globalization today a freewheeling return to Baroque mercantilist anarchy. Upon the Open Pacific in 2021, multinational entities do what they please; and prefer "freeports" rich enough to cater to their every whim; like the ports of LA. Another historical strategy, mostly after 2010, has been to examine urban zones as freeports, then and now (i.e. mercantilist concessions to foreign traders); and the blurred meaning of sovereign urban territory then and now. This runs parallel to post-structural concepts of deterritorialization. It imagines cities reshaped by neo-mercantilism; see, e.g., Easterling; Eldon.

Leiter/Barbour).[17] Contracts from Washington diminished, especially when gridlock overtook Congress after 1994, after Gingrich unleashed the Contract With America. Then nothing much was done after Clinton's Penisgate fiasco started.

Interregnum

Post-Trump America even resembles medieval Byzantium in some ways. Byzantium had once dominated the eastern Mediterranean, including Egypt, but lost out to Arabs, Turks, and to fellow Christians. Constantinople itself was sacked by Trump-like Crusaders in 1204. The Byzantines then drifted into insignificance while Crusaders took over for sixty years, and proceeded to bleed and destroy everything Byzantine. What followed was an interregnum where Constantinople lost colonies to Venice, and in the north, to Russia. By the time the city of Constantinople actually fell in 1453, it had undergone a violent drift lasting 450 years, a population drop of ninety per cent from its peak. That is the mood in the US at large in 2021, quite melodramatic. But is this the end of interregnum, or simply another stage?

The American interregnum is a dialect from the early stages of European imperialism. As empires gradually fade, they produce many dialects – a subaltern overlay of leftovers. These do not simply die; they eccentrically reincarnate, as they fracture into separate regions. The period after the Cold War revived nativist hatreds within the US. That split the nation into three political sovereignties: the Atlantic kingdom, the Pacific kingdom, and the new Confederacy. In the meantime, master planning all but ceased for generations. I leave the reader to guess whether that puts us in 2021 in the second act or the third act. Biden's first two

---

17   The rift between the federal government and LA's regional needs grew much wider after 1980; and especially in the nineties. I do remember FEMA being very helpful after the Northridge Earthquake (1994). But that was also the year of Gingrich's Contract With America, which began a defunding cycle that did not stop until 2021.

years will tell; as will future planning in quasi-sovereign kingdoms like Los Angeles.

The rerouting of LA since 1990 – and not just the ports – is a product of earthshaking proportions. Clearly, nothing will be easily resolved. Our *longue durée* resembles how the Roman empires faded away. Or the Spanish and the Mediterranean empires in the sixteenth century. Or the Ottomans after 1693, or the Ming Dynasty, the Persian kingdoms in Central Asia, or India in the late middle ages. Hyper-powerful empires tend to contract, lose equilibrium. Their decay incubates new civilizations. After the Western hegemony ended, the earth was terraformed again.

The Biden Administration will redirect us away from Trump's suicidal distrust of California. But the overall transition may take fifty years. The elections of 2020 nearly toppled the Constitution itself, with years of unrest to come. America is being transmogrified, that much is certain. Among the possible scenarios is that Americans will take charge of this liquid moment. I vote for that.

The eighties! Where would Trump be without the decade that made him a rock star? Whatever those 1980 fissures have been – economic, racist, technological – they came of age in 2020. And yet, somehow on a micro level: As we paused, they saturated into the fine points of everyday life.

Portability

The matrix radiating from LA Harbor provides a million jobs across four counties, and 2.9 million nationwide (see Flanigan). That means 73% of all cargo in the West Coast, and 30% nationwide, on average over $2 billion a day. The supply chain from China, in particular, is now so continuous, it dissolves many boundaries within the US itself. The increasing congestion at the ports will not stop this blurring of sovereignty.

I was already researching this mutation while I wrote *The History of Forgetting* and *Bleeding Through*. I grew convinced that it is part of what I call a feudal condition, as opposed to a feudal system. That is, the steady hardening of oligarchy weakens the federal government, especially through multinational evasions of the law, and revenue loss (even locally in San Pedro). That loss inspires a growing rage that is damaging the rule of law, safe elections, and long-term planning by the federal government. I imagined Molly's world as part of a growing abscess. A character, Harry Brown, became my avatar for explaining how picaresques and piracies operated inside this world. Then Harry was given his own project, *The Imaginary 20th Century*. But I had been cultivating Harry since 1979. I watched cities being forced to plan independently of the federal government, as regionalism overwhelmed constitutional government.

Neo-mercantilism is feudo-capitalist, a blend of job precarity and multinational neglect of America itself. One might call it America International, rather than America Inc. It has taken Los Angeles over fifty years to adapt, to evolve into a crossroads city, between continents. After 1898, Harry was hired for over fifty years to hide crimes for the oligarchs of Los Angeles.

As of 1970, Los Angeles relied heavily on the militarized federal government (aerospace, research grants, Asian war zones). Since then, various feudo-mercantilist alternatives have stepped in, intensifying the bond with new East Asian economies, and northern Mexico. Even Hollywood, that most American of industries, has grown ever more international, around the Chinese market. The software industries, of course, are a ship with all flags. Global imperatives have transformed Los Angeles from an island on the land to a hanseatic kingdom.

We understand that immigration to Southern California is part of it. But so is our suffocating infrastructure. Intense traffic has broken up the region into hubs of about 800,000 people. Each hub has joined the neo-mercantilist new stage. Downtown is increasingly living off deliveries from the ports. The beach town hub is increasingly absorbing Asian investors, adding to the run-up in the cost of housing. Hollywood increasingly partners with Silicon Valley, which has practically no national boundaries at all. Most of all, housing prices have rocketed. A home is increasingly a neo-mercantilist portfolio, like a manifest off a container ship. These portfolios are easily more international, like the 1930s French concession in old Shanghai. The contrast between overdone global hotel life, and the lumpen class around it has grown. Los Angeles is not London yet, but the parallels are unmistakable, especially in bourgeois rehabs of old warehouse districts (Tribeca vs. the Arts District in LA). In Hollywood, gated communities from the nineties have turned to softcore real estate apartheid, through parking restrictions, and new styles of redlining. A hansa-style soft-power version of glitzy districts continues, while an urban schizophrenia makes police abuses all but impossible to contain. And housing for the homeless remains an insoluble mess.

Road networks are crucial to neo-mercantilism. The keystone that we never see is the Alameda Corridor (1992), dedicated to transporting goods from the ports (at least ten million container units per year). Meanwhile, the American nation state was being steadily dismantled, ever faster after 2010, while I wrote *The Imaginary 20th Century*. Hyperregionalism and urban fracture would soon inspire white supremacism across the country. Signs of political erosion slowed down basic services within city governments, especially resources to fill in the gaps quickly. However, public services inside downtown utterly collapsed.

In the year that I wrote *Bleeding Through*, LA already resembled crossroads cities like Byzantium or even Venice. It operated across continents, even as a sovereign power. Historically, such mercantile kingdoms served as freeports. Even tiny New Amsterdam was almost unrestricted – 2,000 residents, renamed New York after 1660. Freeports must be flexible, more open to strangers. They are also usually open to cultural diversity from outside.

While I worked on *Bleeding Through*, especially its archives, I noticed how automation and AI were changing the street level facts of Los Angeles. At the ports themselves, new waves of automation were already depressing employment. Soon, digital apps would steadily replace people. Both media novels were homages to a future where cities would be dominated by the screen.

Then there is the broader question of how computers will alter the physical city: Clearly, to service the internet of things requires more fulfilment warehouses closer to home, to keep up with e-commerce, through Amazon and FedEx. The logistics sector already accounts for 20% of all new jobs (during the pandemic, higher than that). More light manufacturing goes with more logistics: spare parts, new packaging, 3D printing. Add to that regional (rather than global) factories now asked to deliver renewable energy, like batteries and solar panels. We are about to see an inversion of offshoring and the global. Logistics is outstripping production through overextended bottlenecks. But why is this so fragile all of a sudden? The origins go back to the fifties, when high consumerism took off, to finally account for 70% of the entire economy. The internet merely turned consumer marketing into global logistics. That means light manufacturing in industrial parks and smaller shops, but where is the master plan? On the computer? Who said puppet masters are not your friend (at least on Facebook)? How involuted our madness has become.

Oops. Your screen says that Amazon just delivered a package. Talk about end-to-end visibility and flexible process! (see "Impact of COVID-19"). The pandemic is turning logistics into the last friend who can walk on your front porch. In the years to come, that means shorter supply chains to stay fast; a speedup of trends since 2016. And unfortunately, at the warehouse, that "requires" more robots (and fewer employees) to bring a smile to your face.

Molly's first husband suffered from a mental disease that has recently made a comeback. Thus, *Bleeding Through* is a psychological tool where digitized citizenship leads to melancholia. As Freud insisted (1917–26), melancholia also means grieving for a world lost around you.[18] That grief might zombify you, or drive you into explosive violence. Neither serve citizenship in real terms. Perhaps the US is mutating a different model of national government altogether. Will LA politics

---

18   "Mourning and Melancholia." The reference is to the monumental translation of Freud begun by Virginia Woolf and Leonard Woolf back in the twenties, finally published in toto in the decades after 1953. Since the late nineties, reevaluation of Freud on Mourning has generated many books and articles, from Judith Butler, Derrida, Leo Bersani, Isabell Lorey; reevaluations of Foucault and Benjamin, and of Hegel. The heart of the matter is that flip switch, where a nihilistic zombie-like mourning flashes into rage; also how mourning serves as the bridge where the unconscious is invaded by neo-mercantilism, by the feudal condition.

mutate as well? Clearly, Los Angeles, like other great American cities, remains in drift. Anthropocene evasions keep mounting.

I label these as part of Neo-Mercantilism (globalized paranoias) and emergent urban feudalism (increasing indenture and neighborhood chaos matched by real estate oligarchy). It seems naïve to shrink these grand themes down to cute neighborhoods inside the gig economy – or Molly's three square miles. But power does radiate on to streets. Bland sandwich cafes in modernist office towers are in trouble. With more work at home, neighborhood bars will expand (if they survive the pandemic). Los Angeles will have to frantically house ten percent more poverty; and service another twenty percent who are nearly homeless. Tented hoovervilles (as in the Great Depression) will begin to dot city parks.[19] As I often say, your grandchildren will ask you about 2020.

---

19   The crisis surrounding the closure of a homeless encampment in Echo Park in late March, 2021: 174 tents were removed, and 180 protesters arrested. There is clearly more to come across the LA area. But the future for the unhoused must not be envisioned strictly as a tent. For every homeless person, imagine fifty who are nearly homeless. Then imagine millions of people a paycheck away from being on the street. How will they organize their lives? Sleep in closets, in cars, on trains? Over the next few years surely, rents will skyrocket. Over the next twenty years, the percentage of gig jobs within the labor market will also skyrocket. How many directions will bare survival require? (see Oreskes; Oreskes/Smith). A program for housing the homeless has accelerated slightly in L.A., due to the pandemic (another 6,500 units added in early 2021, with 62,000 already on the waiting list). However, the larger problem must be solved nationally. That is: how to give more people a job and a future, not just a temporary roof over their heads. Since 1974, the precarious economy has been made infinitely worse by a shrunken public sector. As of 2021, the housing shockwave is so far gone, it can only be addressed by Washington first. But that alone could never be enough. The federal response must be coordinated with local bond issues as well; and with cultural reforms across the entire educational sector. And finally, corporations must offer genuine support, as a sound investment. A jobs engine of this kind, both legal and structural, can save perhaps a hundred million Americans from being "nearly homeless" in the future. This is not an impossibly high statistic. As FDR said at his second inaugural address in 1937 (after substantial improvement in the economy), "I see one third of a nation ill-housed, ill-clad, ill-nourished."

Historians will dedicate programs to it. At the same time, children will dress up as Americans for Halloween.

Bibliography

"Editorial: Ghosts of Rampart are hovering over LAPD's latest gang scandal." *LA Times,* Jan 21, 2020.

"Impact of COVID-19 on the World's Logistics Market: Post-Pandemic Growth Opportunity Assessment Report 2020." *Research and Markets* (Global Newswire). June 29, 2020.

Alameda Corridor Project: Its Successes and Challenges, Subcommittee Hearings by the United States Congress, April, 2001 (CreateSpace Independent Publishing Platform, 2018).

Alameda Corridor Transportation Authority. "Completed Projects." https://www.acta.org/about/ projects/completed-projects.

Baker, Bob. "LA's Booming Auto Industry Now a Memory." *LA Times,* July 20, 1991.

Barden, Lane. "The Trench: The Alameda Corridor Picturing Los Angeles." *The Infrastructural City: Networked Ecologies in Los Angeles.* Ed. Kazys Varnelis. Barcelona: Actar, 2009. 238–251.

Bhimji, Fazila. "Struggles, Urban Citizenship, and Belonging: The Experience of Undocumented Street Vendors and Food Truck Owners in Los Angeles." *Urban Anthropology and Studies of Cultural Systems and World Economic Development,* Vol. 39, No. 4. Issue: Informal Economies in North America. Winter, 2010, 455–492.

CBRE. "US Industrial Market Flash: Distribution Hubs Will Benefit from Increased Business Inventories and Supply Chain Restructuring." May 14, 2020.

Chiland, Elijah. "Single-family homes cover almost half of Los Angeles – here's how that happened." *Curbed LA,* Jan. 15, 2020.

Cowan, Jill, Robert Gebeloff. "As Rents Outrun Pay, California Families Live on a Knife's Edge." *New York Times,* Nov. 21, 2019; updated Feb. 12, 2021.

De Lara, Juan. *Inland Shift: Race, Space and Capital in Southern California.* Berkeley: University of California Press, 2018.

Easterling, Keller. *Extrastatecraft: The Power of Infrastructure Space.* London: Verso, 2014.

Eldon, Stuart. *The Birth of Territory.* Chicago: University of Chicago Press, 2013.

Flanigan, James. "Keep on Trucking at the Ports." *LA Times*, Oct. 22, 2003;

Freud, Sigmund. "Mourning and Melancholia." *The Standard Edition of the Complete Psychological Works of Sigmund Freud.* Tr. James Strachey. Volume XIV. London: Hogarth Press/Institute of Psycho-Analysis, 1957. 243–258.

Global Supply Chains Research Group. "China Supply Chain Inquiry Report-back." Dec. 5, 2015.

Glover, Scott, Matt Lait. "Evidence Backs Majority of Perez's Allegations of Wrongdoing." *LA Times*, Aug. 11, 2003.

Gold, Jonathan. "How America Became a Food Truck Nation (tracing the food truck revolution back to its Los Angeles roots)." *Smithsonian Magazine*, March 2012.

Gottlieb, Robert. "Port of Call: On Becoming China's Entrepôt." *Boom: A Journal of California*, Vol. 5, No. 1, Spring 2015, 29–37.

Johnson, Eric. "Container gateways evolving from cargo ports to data portals." *JOC – Journal of Commerce online.* Mar. 02, 2020.

Kezar, Adrianna, Tom DePaola, Daniel T. Scott. *The Gig Academy: Mapping Labor in the Neoliberal University.* Baltimore: Johns Hopkins University Press, 2019.

Kirham, Chris. "Growth in Inland Empire soars; The region is forecast to lead the Southland in the rate of job and business creation." *LA Times*, Oct. 23, 2014.

Lee, Nathaniel. "How police militarization became an over $5 billion business coveted by the defense industry." CNBC, July 10, 2020.

Leiter, Robert, Elissa Barbour. "Regional Planning in Southern California." *Planning Los Angeles.* Ed. David. C. Sloane. Chicago: Planners Press, 2012. 162–170.

Levy, Stephen. *Insanely Great: The Life and Times of Macintosh, the Computer that Changed Everything.* London: Penguin Books, 2000.

Lopez, Robert. "Vendors Demand a Hearing at City Hall." *LA Times*, August 1, 1993.

Lopez, Robert. "Vendors Protest against LAPD." *LA Times*, Aug. 2, 1994.

Macias Jr., Martin. "Furusato: The Lost Japanese Fishing Village Between LA's Ports." *Courthouse News Service*, June 12, 2018.

Meares, Hadley. "Off the coast of San Pedro, a Japanese community erased: Isolated from the mainland of Los Angeles, Fish Harbor was a 'dreamland' until 1942."*la.curbed*, March 30, 2018.

Mongelluzzo, Bill. "LA port taps $7.5 million to reward productive terminals." *JOC – Journal of Commerce online*, Jan. 21, 2021.

Oreskes, Benjamin, Doug Smith. "How a commune-like encampment in Echo Park became flashpoint in L.A.'s homelessness crisis." *LA Times*, March 13, 2021.

Oreskes, Benjamin. "City plans to close Echo Park Lake and clear homeless encampment." *LA Times*, March 23, 2021.

Peralta, Christian. "Back to the Future: The 1970 Los Angeles 'Centers' Concept Plan." *Planetizen*, April 5, 2007.

Puko, Timothy. "In Los Angeles, an Economy Built on Freelancers Crumbles: Creative workers with multiple gigs are among the worst hit by the recession and face long roads to recovery." *Wall Street Journal*, June 20, 2020.

Rampart Area Corruption Incident (Public Report, 371 pages), Board of Inquiry, LAPD, March 1, 2000.

Regardie, Jon. "After COVID-19, Can Downtown L.A. Get Back Up?" *Los Angeles Magazine*, March 24, 2021.);

Resnick, Rose. "When Foodie Met Truckie: The Story of Food Trucks in LA." *Thrillist*, Jan, 16, 2016.

Roberts, Bill. "Production in View: Allan Sekula's Fish Story and the Thawing of Postmodernism." *Tate (Museum) Papers*, No. 18, Autumn 2012.

Sanchez, Jesus. "High and Dry: Downtown Struggles to Recover From 1980s Building Boom That Went Bust." *LA Times*, Oct. 15, 1995.

Scott, Allen J. "The Aerospace-Electronics Industrial Complex of Southern California: The Formative Years, 1940–1960." *Research Policy*, Vol. 20, No. 5, Oct. 1991, 439–456.

Sharpsteen, Bill. *The Docks*. Berkeley: University of California Press, 2011.

Strange, Susan. *Casino Capitalism*. Manchester: Manchester University Press, 1997 [¹1986].

Tirschwell, Peter. "Solution Elusive to Avoid Next LA–LB Port Backup." *JOC – Journal of Commerce online*, March 19, 2021.

Trinh, Jean. "LA's Food Truck Boom Happened 10 Years Ago: Where Are They Now." *Eater Los Angeles*, Sept. 13, 2018.

Vartabedian, Ralph. "Northrop to Cut 3,000 from Work Force." *Los Angeles Times*, March 25, 1994.

Waldinger, Roger, Mehdi Bozorgmehr. *Ethnic Los Angeles*. New York: Russell Sage Foundation, 1996.

Waters, Tim. "San Pedro Fishermen, Hurt by Closing of Canneries, Want to Buy One of Their Own: Boat Owners Seek Deal With Star-Kist." *LA Times*, March 9, 1987.

Webster, John. "Home Sweet PC." *Computerworld*, April 1, 1991.

Weinstein, Henry. "Rampart Probe May Now Affect Over 3,000 Cases." *LA Times*, Dec. 15, 1999.

White, Ronald. "Soaring Port Traffic Delivers More Jobs: A boom in trade and cargo volume has turned the docks in L.A. and Long Beach into an employment engine." *LA Times*, July 19, 2004.

Zamicho, Nora. "Wilson OKs Use of Eminent Domain to Create Railway Corridor: Transit: Governor urges that condemnation be used only as a last resort in talks with Southern Pacific, which wants $260 million for its route between Downtown and the Harbor area." *LA Times*, Sept. 9, 1993.

Bleeding Through: 'The Making of'

5. "The Unreliable Narrator"
The kernel of Molly's story in a docufable

Norman M. Klein

Years ago, I knew a 93-year-old lady named Molly Frankel, who owned a battered Queen Ann Victorian house, about five years older than she was, on what was once a fancy corner lot just north of Carroll Avenue, in Angelino Heights. She had moved in somewhere between 1919 and 1928; had survived two husbands, one a possible suicide. No one knew the details for certain; or at least her relatives who might know wouldn't say. Even Molly didn't seem to have essential facts straight.

"My husband was a sporting man," she used to explain, meaning a smart dresser, a john for prostitutes, or a gambler. "I came to Los Angeles in 1928, right after the war, and got a job as a bookkeeper. His father saw I was a hard worker, running their business. So he more or less forced his son to settle down with me. I wasn't much to look at, but he knew I would help his boy stay at home more."

"Did you?"

Molly laughed, remembering something intimate or embarrassing about her first husband. Then she added: "Now my second husband I kept saying no to. He asked me to marry him five times a week. I exaggerate. He said to me once. He was a lawyer for my business. He says to me: 'We could organize very well together.'"

"So?"

"So he was home continuously."

Molly still ran her shop, located somewhere in the warehouse district on Main, near the flophouses. She sold "inside felt" that was used for the collars on suits. "I get my best sleep there," she said.

One Fourth of July, her grand-niece, who now lives in Vegas, came by to drive her to a party. Molly wore her better wig, had her beaded purse. But she was confused somehow by the entire event.

The next day, a Sunday, I saw Molly ambling down the hill at dusk, toward the bus. Then she realized her mistake, and told me: "I must have overslept. I missed a day somehow."

She was beginning to lose track of the difference between sunrise and sunset. Having just had her driver's license revoked, she would take the Temple Street bus into downtown, then get her store ready, waiting for the sun to come up, until finally it was clear that either there was a solar eclipse or she'd missed a day somehow.

Molly lived on the second floor and rented out the rest to a large Mexican family. They seemed desperate to keep Molly around, because she never raised the rent, and they knew that her family coveted her property. I was invited to visit Molly once at her house, and found her seated in the kitchen, making toast over the stove, using a forties vintage wire toaster that sat on the gas burner. Her built-in cupboards were bulging with depression glass – pink and rose dishes crammed so tight that they were about to spring the lock. Up in her attic – some 1,200 square feet of raw space – I found, hidden behind a lateral support beam, a dusty brown bag tied with rope. I asked her what this was, and she shrugged, but said I could have it if I wanted. Inside were four books from the W.E.B. Du Bois Club – imprints from the early thirties. Was Molly a thirties Socialist?

"Must have been my sister. She was the reader."

"This has been here for fifty years. Was your sister involved in politics?"

"I don't go up here much."

Later I found out that her husband, apparently the organized one, had hanged himself up in the attic. But no one could say for certain.

Across the street, inside a huge Craftsman house, another of the matrons in the neighborhood had died in her late seventies, and left all her clothing stacked neatly, like fossil sediment, one on top of the other, from 1918 as a Temperance activist to 1983. Apparently, the living room was large enough to hold over three hundred people at her niece's wedding in the early fifties. Now her niece's daughter, a very serious young nurse, had moved in to keep the family interest going – just her and her boyfriend in 7,500 square feet.

The neighbors told her to listen for ghosts. Then after a few weeks, apparently, a rattle developed up in her attic. It would wake her up at night. Finally, out of purely secular desperation for a good night's sleep, she walked up the attic steps and asked her dead aunt for a truce. I'll keep the door closed up here, she offered, if you'll stop waking me up at night. And that was enough apparently.

One early evening I saw Molly on her way to the Temple Street bus again. I stopped her, and insisted that it was sundown. She laughed at me, but agreed to wait long enough to find out. Then, as the sky darkened and the night breezes started, she finally apologized, saying that ever since that Fourth of July party last month she kept getting her days mixed up.

That was about ten years ago. Molly's family took the house, and put her in a senior citizen's home, where she grew enormously fat, and may have been happy for all I know. She died five years later, apparently older than she admitted to, somewhere around a hundred.

It must be strange to live in a world that utterly transforms around you, as if you were an immigrant in your own house. As I explained earlier, from 1928 (or 1919), the area went from mixed Anglo and Jewish bourgeois to prostitutes and drug dealers down the corner in the early seventies. On Sunset Boulevard, there had once been gyms where the young Anthony Quinn trained to be a boxer in the thirties, then thought better of it, and worked on Sundays in the church of Sister Aimee Semple McPherson. Not a whisper of all that remains, except the Jensen center, which had declined into a drug contact by the late fifties, and had long since turned its bowling alleys into discount stores.

There are practically no fragments left of Molly's life, and certainly no memories in the house, which has since been sold and renovated into upscale apartments. I have no idea how I would find out precisely where Molly lied. "I hide a few years," she used to say. I don't even really know if her life was dowdy or melodramatic. Like that of the Vietnamese whom I interviewed, hers is a history of ways to distract information more than erase it.

That is more or less the spirit of unreliable narrator. It is a story based on how we forget or repress memory.[1] Clearly it has a literary

---

1   Ways of Lying – a few narrative devices involving an unreliable narrator: a) Announcing the mental weakness of the character within the first paragraph (usually in the first person) as symptomatic of an affliction, or as the moment after unsettling sleep, when the dream cannot be shaken loose yet. For example, Gogol's Poprishchin in "Diary of a Madman" has trouble waking up to get to work, and seems disoriented still as he walks into the dreary Russian cold. In Kafka's *Metamorphosis*, in the third person, of course, the symptom is identified in the first line. Or take the opening of the novel *The Blind Owl* by Iranian master Sadegh Hedayat (1903–1951): "There are sores which slowly erode the mind in solitude like a kind of canker." And, of course, the model openings in Poe and from Dostoyevsky's *Notes from Underground*. b) When the narrator "writes" unreliable entries directly on the imaginary page. The classic example is Gogol's "Diary of a Madman", where Poprishchin loses control of his diary when he can write 'Spain' only as the word 'China': "China and Spain are really one and the same country... If you don't believe me, then try to write 'Spain,' and you'll end up writing 'China.'" And, of course, the many tricks of misremembering on the page that Sterne performs. c) When the narrator clearly refuses to discuss a crucial event that the reader senses. This is very typical of the caricature of the novel of sociability in eighteenth-century literature. In noir fiction, this device allows the murderer to feel morally justified, while the reader senses that this denial will come home to roost. Deleuze and Guattari identify this hiding of events as "fundamental forgetting," "the nothing that makes us say 'whatever could have happened to make me forget where I put my keys, or whether I have mailed that letter?'" The characters have forgotten something that must be fundamental, because they seem lost without it. See also Deleuze and Guattari's chapter on the novella in *A Thousand Plateaus*: the evacuated pre-history that is essential to the novella (the forgotten diegesis); the events that are a phantom presence, but that no character chooses to remember (narrate to us). Kleist's play *Prince Frederick of Homburg* is an interesting case of whether the fundamental forgetting is willful or involuntary. The director of any performance of the play must decide whether the prince is dreaming or not, because the character is never allowed to know. d) Hurricane in the eye: once the unreliable parameters are established in the story, no matter how outrageous these are, they must exist in a world of absolute verisimilitude, as in Gregor Samsa's household (*Metamorphosis*), or the

tradition behind it: from eighteenth-century fiction in particular (the Münchhausens and Uncle Tobys); in Russian literature after Gogol's short stories[2]; German and Central European fiction after 1880[3]; the Romantic fascination with demolished historic places as unreliable narrators, the absent presence that in Michelet's words are "obscure and dubious witnesses" (1847; see Orr).[4] Virginia Woolf's emptied rooms where the remains of memory are displaced[5]; American tall tales that Mark Twain loved; in Roland Barthes's S/Z; in noir fiction by Jim Thompson or David Goodis, where the narrator is a criminal who has to repress what he does, and lie to the reader[6]; in the broad crisis of representation in cinema (see Stam et al. 97–103)[7] that I discuss in the next section [of

---

responses to the runaway nose in Gogol's story. e) Interruptions: as if to suggest something too painful to remember but essential to the story; possibly to shift the blame for something the reader cannot know. In that sense, much stream-of-consciousness fiction uses the unreliable narrator: the deliberately erased story that the narrator wants to explain but will omit. f) The matter of degree: obviously these devices appear to some degree in all fiction. In some cases, however, they dominate the structure and the chain of events.

2   Gogol's "Diary of a Madman" and "The Nose" are the classic format – the junction between Romantic irony and modernist collage – repeated in Dostoyevsky's "The Crocodile," in Kafka's Metamorphosis, and in absurdist fiction and theater of the fifties.

3   A particular favorite of mine, gruesome I admit, is the short story "The Autopsy," by Georg Heym (1887–1912), German Expressionist poet, playwright, and novelist. A dead man is losing memory while the doctor does an autopsy.

4   For a critique of historical culture, see Partner.

5   Woolf's "A Haunted House" is among the most abbreviated examples I know.

6   Also in novels about amnesiacs, like Cornell Woolrich's The Black Curtain.

7   For the following, see Stam et al., 97–104: Borrowing from the writings of Genette, the unreliable narrator in film is defined usually as one type of voice-over: the "embedded" narrator – one of the characters who is embedded in the action. The embedded narrator then becomes a subset of the "intra-diegetic" narrator: any form of interior voice-over. For the story to "work," the audience must sense that these voices are "unreliable," that the intra (insider) narrator has a stake in lying, may not "see straight" in the heat of the moment. In opposition to this "intra" variant is the "extra-diegetic." "Extra," as in outside: a voice-over from a character not in the scene, who provides exposition primar-

History of Forgetting] (how film about Los Angeles distracts the real space; the unreliability of television as political memory).

"In old apartments," writes Bruno Schulz, speaking through the voice of a father, "there are rooms which are sometimes forgotten. Unvisited for months on end, they wilt between the walls and ... close in on themselves" (67–68). The Father went inside one of these collapsed rooms, and found that "slim shoots grow [in the crevices] ... filling the gray air with a scintillating filigree lace of leaves." But by nightfall, they are "gone without a trace." "The whole elusive sight was a fata morgana, an example of the strange make-believe of matter which had created a semblance of life."

---

ily. Among the films usually cited in this discussion are: Hitchcock's *Stage Fright* (the "lying flashback"); Resnais's *Last Year at Marienbad*; Weir's *Breaker Morant*; Kurosawa's *Rashomon*; Altman's *Fool for Love*; Buñuel's *That Obscure Object of Desire*. When *Laura* is cited, that brings to mind another cache of films altogether, to which I would add *Usual Suspects* (1995) – stories where a suspect's memory of a crime is re-enacted from voice-over, but proves to be a red herring, or a lie. Among film theory cited are: Sarah Kozloff *Invisible Storytellers* (1988); Seymour Chatman, *Story and Discourse* (1978); Francesco Casetti, *D'un regard l'autre* (1986); and essays on Hitchcock; Guido Fink on *Laura* and *Mildred Pierce*. However, in this project, I found the omissions by voice-over and flashback more appropriate. For example, Barthes in *Image–Music–Text* suggests how props and the gaps between characters imply unreliable memory. Another useful form is how short-term memory operates as montage in experimental cinema – the appropriation or the repetition of familiar texts as loops in films, e.g. Rybczinski's *Tango*. I also would consider Buñuel's "documentary" *Land Without Bread* very much an "unreliable" use of denotation. The extra-diegetic voice-over, usually a manly baritone, is "lying." He contradicts with surgical precision what is undeniably real footage by Buñuel's crew – of a truly miserable cluster of towns known as Las Hurdes in Spain. Finally in this partial list: all forms of "upside-down" animation are unreliable narrators, e.g. the animated cartoon – see my *Seven Minutes: The Life and Death of the American Animated Cartoon*. By upside-down, I mean gravity upside down, spatiality upside down, customs upside down (e.g., Tex Avery), as opposed to barely noticed mattes in live action, or heads inserted digitally on another body.

Bibliography

Barthes, Roland. *Image–Music–Text*. New York: Hill & Wang, 1977.

Deleuze, Gilles, Félix Guattari. *A Thousand Plateaus*. Trans. Brian Massumi. London, New York: Continuum, 2004 [¹1987]. Vol. 2 of *Capitalism and Schizophrenia*. 2 vols. 1972–1980. 3–28. [Trans. of *Mille Plateaux*. Paris : Editions de Minuit, 1980].

Hedayat, Sadegh. *The Blind Owl*. Trans. D.P. Costello. New York: Grove Weidenfeld, 1957.

Klein, Norman M. *Seven Minutes: The Life and Death of the American Animated Cartoon*. London: Verso, 1993.

Orr, Linda. "Intimate Images: Subjectivity and History – Stael, Michelet and Tocqueville." *A New Philosophy of History*. Ed. Frank Ankersmit, Hans Kellner. Chicago: University of Chicago Press, 1995. 89–107.

Partner, Nancy. "Historicity in an Age of Reality-Fictions." *A New Philosophy of History*. Ed. Frank Ankersmit, Hans Kellner. Chicago: University of Chicago Press, 1995. 21–39.

Schulz, Bruno. *The Street of Crocodiles*. Trans. C. Wieniewska. New York: Penguin Books, 1977 [orig. 1934].

Stam, Robert, Robert Burgoyne, Sandy Flitterman-Lewis. *New Vocabularies in Film Semiotics: Structuralism, Post-Structuralism and Beyond*. London: Routledge, 1992.

6. "Noir as the Ruins of the Left"
A docufable on Walter Benjamin in Los Angeles

Norman M. Klein

Mike Davis has occasionally thought about writing a piece tentatively entitled "Walter Benjamin in Boyle Heights." Benjamin does not commit suicide; instead he takes the boat to New York and winds up among the German émigrés in Los Angeles. Being too much a scholar of the city street, he elects not to live in the Pacific Palisades, not to bow at the feet of Thomas Mann. But he does show up at modified barbecues at Feuchtwanger's[1] estate, chats with Schoenberg, and hopes for some beneficence from Mann, for the phone call that could bring a hefty literary contract perhaps, anything to improve the pittance that the Frankfurt School in Exile provides. (I can feel myself embroidering here.) Benjamin moves instead to Boyle Heights, a Jewish/Mexican/Japanese/Serb enclave just east of downtown, across a bridge that reminds him of bridges in Berlin perhaps. After a somewhat tortured version of a power lunch with Bertolt Brecht, he decides to write a *Chronik* on Hollywood studios, particularly those at Gower Gulch, the marginal ones that produce horse operas and cheesy Flash Gordon serials.

Benjamin takes the Sunset Red Car to Gower, feels his suit in need of pressing under the baking, dry heat, but walks another mile until the

---

1   Lion Feuchtwanger, whose home in Pacific Palisades (at Paso Robles) was the literary meeting place for the German writers in exile (interview with Richard Hertz, 1995).

Crossroads to the World[2] display catches his eye. A globe of the planet, continents included, spins serenely and idiotically in front of a patch of stores, and what might resemble an arcade (there is also an arcade in downtown Los Angeles). But he feels too far away from all that shopping history to bother anymore. All his notes are crated somewhere in Paris, probably being used as briquettes for heating a flat in the winter.

Years later, a scholar tries to interpret the writings of Walter Benjamin in Los Angeles. Apparently, Benjamin became very interested in meeting Harry Raymond, the detective who had cracked open the Shaw Administration downtown, forced it out of office, to be replaced by the reform mayor Fletcher Bowron. Raymond, who still lived in Boyle Heights just blocks from Benjamin, had survived being blown up by a bomb planted in his car by Earl Kytelle. Later, after continued threats on his life, he "blew the lid off of City Hall" in a very steamy trial.

Benjamin also ate at Clifton's cafeteria downtown, and met the owner, Clifford Clinton, formerly an employer of Harry Raymond, for a very politically explicit radio program back in the thirties. Benjamin spoke with him for a while about radio itself, about the shows each had written (Benjamin had worked in radio in the late twenties in Germany). But, most of all, Benjamin had trouble addressing the ruins, allegories and street energy of Los Angeles, the intricacies of its local politics. Flâneurship took on a disengaged spirit, until he located his subject.

---

2   The actual name was Crossroads *of* the World (Benjamin's problem with English – at first). This was a complex built in 1936–37, along Sunset Boulevard in Hollywood, as "an outstanding landmark and civic attraction as well as a centralized shopping district." It was generally perceived more as a "stage set than most retail facilities of any sort." Each building had a national theme: England, France, the Netherlands, Spain, Persia, Colonial New England, etc. It also had a midway, like a fair or a carny; and the project overall was continuously advertised as the first consumer space to function immediately as a public space as well, however exaggerated the sense of 'public'. Benjamin missed many of these details, but saw it as a composite of "American Surrealist evasion," and found the French simulacrum a bit "terrifying, along with what they thought passed for coffee" (see Longstreth 792ff.).

I can see him taking notes in a movie theater, taking in the used book-stores on Third Street, working as a tutor, trying once again to position himself within a university. His study on B films as baroque irony took four years to write, while he drifted uneasily inside the margins of the German/noir film community. His descriptions of walking through La Cienega Boulevard undoubtedly influenced Sartre's visit to L.A. right af-ter the war, and Sartre's essay "American Cities," where he declared in somewhat omniscient fashion that neither New York nor Chicago had neighborhoods in the purer European sense, and that streets in America were generally nothing more than "a piece of highway."

> In certain cities I noticed a real atrophy of the sidewalk. In Los Ange-les, for example, on La Cienega, which is lined with bars, theaters, restaurants, antique dealers and private residences, the sidewalks are scarcely more than side-streets that lead customers and guests from the roadway into the house. Lawns have been planted from the façades to the roadway of this luxurious avenue. I followed a narrow path between the lawns for a time without meeting a living soul, while to my right, cars streaked by on the road; all animation in the street had taken refuge on the high road. (Sartre 123).

Benjamin actually filed this quotation in 1956, a few months before his death. Beside it, he wrote, in that clipped style he developed later in his life: "A city is a blind courier. It brings nothing. It takes nothing. That is why we grow so fixated on roads. Sartre should have watched the dust settle more."

The scholar found this inside fifty pages of notes for a Los Angeles *Passagenwerk* – nothing as elaborate as what Benjamin planned to write about the Parisian arcades. But on page 14 Benjamin had circled the same quotation from his writing that Davis used, quite coincidentally, as the preface to *City of Quartz*:

> The superficial inducement, the exotic, the picturesque has an ef-fect only on the foreigner. To portray a city, a native must have other, deeper motives – motives of one who travels into the past instead of

into the distance. A native's book about his city will always be related to memoirs; the writer has not spent his childhood there in vain.[3]

The term "memoir" is the link; more specifically, the memoir of buildings inhabited by political ghosts. In Benjamin's writings about Berlin and Paris, city streets resemble what he defined as ruin in his first book *The Origin of German Tragic Drama*. Ruins are shells of faded memory recovered as theater – stylized, aestheticized; an exotic memory of distilled torment. No matter how authentic the ruin, it is received, or read, as simulated memory: phantasmagoria, dioramas, arcades. Every building is faintly warped to the eye, as if by glaucoma. The built environment is both political critique and nostalgia. So also is his literary style; the montage of quotations on the surface of the page draws attention to the quotations he finds on the surface of buildings.

The memoir then is a contradiction. It describes actions taken, but in the spirit of lost opportunities – deeds left unfinished, barely desired any longer; moments when the writer was a flâneur. As a somewhat metaphysically inclined Marxist, Benjamin was very aware of how paradoxical this approach was[4], as is Mike Davis for that matter, by no means a metaphysician, but often, in his own words, a "reteller of the Book of Apocalypse." In that spirit, I can imagine Benjamin inserting this quotation in his archive about Los Angeles:

---

3   The passage is from Benjamin's 1929 review of Franz Hessel's *Spazieren in Berlin*, entitled "Die Wiederkehr des Flaneurs", known in English as "The Return of the Flaneur". Here quoted from Davis's book.

4   Benjamin describes this contradiction clearly in his oft-cited essay on Surrealists as "profane illuminators." The surrealist use of optical paradox reminds Benjamin of the crisis among revolutionary intelligentsia during the 1920s: "We penetrate the mystery only to the degree that we recognize it in the everyday world, by virtue of a dialectical optic that perceives the everyday as impenetrable, the impenetrable as everyday... Nowhere do ... metaphor and image collide so drastically and so irreconcilably as in politics ... This image sphere, however, can no longer be measured out by contemplation... [That is why] the revolutionary intelligentsia ... has failed almost entirely in making contact with the proletarian masses, because [its imagery] can no longer be performed contemplatively." (*Reflections* 190f.).

Language clearly shows that memory is not an instrument for exploring the past but its theater. It is the medium of past experience, as the
ground is the medium in which dead cities lay interred. (*Reflections*
25f.)[5]

Davis was aware when he wrote *City of Quartz* that much in the language
of academic history functions as "dead cities interred." Its reliquary
function helps distract, rather than spark urban politics. He did not
want a style that divided him from deeply held commitments, centrally
to the labor movement, but to others as well – the politics that evolved
into the gang truce; architectural *charrettes* that occasionally change city
policy; more broadly to political journalism for newspapers or for the
Nation. He therefore chose an activist writing style for *City of Quartz*
– the historian using elements of noir fiction and polemical criticism
– to build an imaginary lively enough to compete with the sunshine
mystique of L.A. promotion. He wanted the book to cut more deeply
into muscle tissue, and perhaps make some political difference.

That is not to say that this style is immune to the crisis that Benjamin
describes, when history "seize[s] hold of a memory as it flashes up at a
moment of danger" ("Theses" 255). Any critique that uses a noir aesthetic
can transform the agonies of the inner city into an exotic descent. On
one level at least, that of popular memory, there is no such thing as bad
publicity for the crimes of capitalism, any more than there is for porno-
graphy.

The popular success of *City of Quartz* has bred an exotic reading that
resembles a cyber-noir opera. There seems no way to avoid that. In the
minds of many fans of the book – certainly the many students who
speak to me – "Fortress L.A." flashes internally like a movie scenario.
Despite its effect on local journalism and on urban studies generally,
that paramnesiac imaginary seems impossible to shake. Students describe helicopters pulsating beneath a huge crane shot. A futuristic swat
team crashes through a window, as if from a *Die Hard* scenario.

---

5   *Berliner Chronik* was started in 1932.

William Gibson, at the back of his novel *Virtual Light*, cites Davis as a singular influence. "His observations regarding the privatization of public space" (Gibson 351f.) can be seen in the character Rydell's life in Los Angeles. Rydell is a rent-a-cop who works for the IntenSecure company, which also specializes in "gated residential" policing, particularly out in the "edge cities" (Gibson 77f.), clearly a term that is part of a much larger debate that includes Davis (cf. Klein ch.2, fn 27). I could not say precisely if other cyber novelists have worked directly with Davis's critique. If they have, their stories would seem to merge two contraries that he discusses: upscale enclaving, and the boom in prisons and surveillance. Novels like Stephenson's *Snow Crash* do happen to resemble Davis's version of the panoptical, as expressed in 1990. One can even sense elements of "Fortress L.A." in the staging of the movie version of *Johnny Mnemonic*. It is a vision of opportunities shattered, of saving democracy after it has died, in a world twenty years after passages from Davis like the following:

> Anyone who has tried to take a stroll at dusk through a strange neighborhood patrolled by armed security guards and signposted with death threats quickly realizes how merely notional, if not utterly obsolete, is the old idea of the "freedom of the city." (250)[6]

I also see a secondary reading of "Fortress L.A.", less essential perhaps. In phrases about the "obsolescence of freedom," Davis's text becomes an ironic confession about political activist literature in the 1990s. American politics at the moment leaves a lot to feel nostalgic about. To some degree, the left is also a phantom limb, much as I regret to say it. Conservative promotion has matured much faster than leftist literature. Our political culture has been emulsified by advertising. Policies and politics continue to skew deeply to the right. And the arc has not turned to the

---

6   Let us examine this image in an innocent way. As a child, I used to wander through Coney Island day and night, watch people knock each other around, hear the groans of prostitutes under the boardwalk, and yet feel immune, as if I had a right to drift through the city. That would seem quite risky for my son, and he instinctively knows it.

left yet. In response, activist literature has begun to take on a baroque theatricality, such that Benjamin used when describing the cultural politics of the twenties and thirties in Western Europe. He sensed, as many on the left do today, that mass promotion had become thorough enough to be a civilization like the Baroque; it delivers its own policies and politics. And while Benjamin was hardly as cynical about this effect as Adorno, he felt its phantoms very personally. They spoke to his own predicament while in exile, an activism distracted, partly erased – like noir literature in yet another way. It is the "detective" describing vagrancy and marginalization, the Jewish Communist intellectual waiting in Paris during an emergent Nazi era.

The linkage in my fictional essay has gone from Benjamin to Davis, and back to noir nostalgia, and finally to cyber-noir. Descriptions of the city street as ruin are at the core of each of these. Benjamin was not deeply involved in noir fiction when he lived in L.A., but he did collect a few quotations from the *Black Mask* school, mostly the moody openings to stories about the climate, particularly the dry winds, driving people to crime. They described for him ruins in the making, similar, he noted, to "the curling wallpaper in my tiny kitchen." One citation came from the story "Goldfish," written by Raymond Chandler in 1936, who was at a low point financially at the time (perhaps Benjamin empathized):

> I wasn't doing any work that day, just catching up on my foot-dangling. A warm gusty breeze was blowing in at the office window and the soot from the Mansion House Hotel oilburners across the alley was rolling across the glass top of my desk in tiny particles, like pollen drifting over a vacant lot. (Chandler, 1st parag.)[7]

That is very much the mood of Chandler interiors, memory dissolving at the edges, like old wallpaper. "I'll Be Waiting" appears in the *Saturday Evening Post* on 14 October 1939, only a month after the start of the war in Europe:

---

7   This is the opening paragraph of "Goldfish", cited in many editions now (e.g., *Trouble is My Business*, originally in *Black Mask* (1936), and reprinted in the Chandler anthology *Red Wind*.

> At one in the morning, Carl, the night porter, turned down the last of three table lamps in the main lobby of the Windermere Hotel.[8] The blue carpet darkened a shade or two and the walls drew back into remoteness. The chairs filled with shadowy loungers. In the corners were memories like cobwebs.

The most prescient symbol that Benjamin collected was about the Santa Ana winds, in what probably has now become the most famous Chandler opening, from "Red Wind" (1938):

> There was a desert wind blowing that night. It was one of those hot dry Santa Anas that come down through the mountain passes and curl your hair and make your nerves jump and your skin itch. On nights like that every booze party ends in a fight. Meek little wives feel the edge of the carving knife and study their husbands' necks. Anything can happen. You can even get a full glass of beer at a cocktail lounge. (Chandler 1938).[9]

In the sixties, this passage was made famous in Joan Didion's *Slouching Toward Bethlehem*[10], a bit of dark flânerie in its own right. But more important to an understanding of what Benjamin sensed, these winds are mentioned by other writers of Chandler's era. Simmering hatreds gather in an uncanny stillness. Ozymandias waits for a dust storm. The dryness is faintly stinging, like a slightly sour amphetamine. (I actually love the Santa Ana sensation, by the way.)

---

8   Years ago, a student made a film about this short story. He began by asking for advice about locations, and found a hotel intact from the thirties. He was disappointed though. It wasn't "dark" enough. I told him that a white, neo-classicist look was very trendy in hotel interiors back then. He remained unconvinced. It simply wasn't "real" enough.

9   See note 7 above. I rarely find an L.A. crime novel that does not mention the Santa Anas somewhere, particularly since 1990 (e.g. Michael Connelly, Alex Abella).

10   The section that mentions Chandler and the winds originally appeared in *The Saturday Evening Post* as "The Santa Ana."

In 1941, Benjamin clipped a section written by Erle Stanley Gardner, then one of the veteran L.A. *Black Mask* writers. It was an extraordinary two pages on santanas. Before they strike, the sky glows with a "startling clarity," "dustless," the air "listless devoid of life." Then the blast of heat "churns up particles of dust so fine they filter between dry lips, grit against the surface of the teeth." (Fair 19f.). The narrator in the story is a writer at work when the dust hits. He has to shutter the windows, but hears the crackle and rattling. His nerves get edgier. The narrative hook has been established, like an undertow. The story begins – in this case about clues to a murder that can be seen in female accessories left on the furniture. A woman appears suddenly in the room, and startles the writer. While the santana continues, she begins to talk about a pair of leather gloves[11] that the writer notices have an inexplicable but telling graphite stain in the corner. (I can't write this without thinking of the gloves in the O.J. Simpson trial being "extra large" but too small, presumably shrunk because they were soaked in blood: another empty trope in that ludicrous trial. Descriptions of trials remain a continual source of threnodic irony in crime books, even parody. Justice is turned into a theatricalized ruin, like the edgy testimony of a hostile witness in a crime film.)

Noir literature emerged in the twenties during many such cases – during the Teapot Domes of the Republican era, during Prohibition, in the vacuum after the Progressive movement was wiped out immediately after the First World War. It was social realism as baroque; leftist activist intentions faintly remembered, then re-enacted with futile results. The crime stories that appeared in *Black Mask* magazine bore out this ambivalence – militant tales about grotesque waste of life, red harvests. The

---

11   Also: the photo of gloves in André Breton's surrealist novel *Nadja* (1927, 57): an aleatory clue to a badly remembered event – in this paramnesiac satire of the gothic. *Nadja* is a prelude to Robbe-Grillet's *The Erasers (Les Gommes,* 1953), where American noir is clearly a source. Again, the clues lead to a circle of undetection, then in the final scene mutually eradicate memory of any crime at all. And note Robbe-Grillet's pun – *gomme* as gummy eraser and the gumshoe (as eraser). Both are "a soft crumbly eraser that friction does not twist but reduces to dust" (Robbe-Grillet 126).

writing generally retains that divided spirit into the thirties, both militant and wistful, despite the enthusiasms of the New Deal – more as a statement about the Depression. It is hard-boiled nostalgia, hinting at periods of moral clarity that have become vestigial in characters like the Continental Op, the Thin Man, or Philip Marlowe. They all booze about a past they cannot entirely forget. And while they have, in Chandler's words, "a disgust for sham and a contempt for pettiness," their world is a withering joke.

> It is not a fragrant world, but it is the world you live in ... It is not funny that a man should be killed, but it is sometimes funny that he should be killed for so little. (Chandler 1972, 21)[12]

After they finish with the crooks, and the dust has settled, the crime remains to some degree past the point of no return. The corpse will not be brought back to life.[13] The evil is still in the atmosphere. Often no one seems all that interested in seeing the crime solved anyway. The decisions that could have made for an easy solution were allowed to lapse. The crime scene is also a ruin. The detective suffers a phantom urge for moral correction, like a bout of malaria. It is a nostalgia for activism during deeply treacherous conservative eras.

---

12   I should add that Chandler's politics did veer to the right, as one might expect for a former oil executive; but always very nostalgically, as if out of disgust for lost chances more than as a commitment to anything resembling the right-wing politics of the forties and fifties, which he generally felt were a pox to the life of the writer. He also found postwar Los Angeles too scrubbed and artificial, even while he is so remorseless in his stories about the decayed districts of prewar Los Angeles. Chandler flourishes in ambience, from the Latin *ambiens*, meaning to "go round," not very far from another Latin root, *ambigere* (as in ambiguity), "to wander."

13   This point brings me to the oddness of the film *Laura* (1944), where the corpse is essentially brought back to life, but the life of the woman who actually was shot to death by mistake, while opening a door, disappears and is barely noted – yet another variation of distraction used as a story hook in crime films, like *Vertigo* (1958), or even *The Third Man* (1949).

Bibliography

Benjamin, Walter. "Theses on the Philosophy of History." *Illuminations*. Ed. Hannah Arendt, trans. Harry Zohn. New York: Schocken Books, 1969 [¹1955), 253–264.

Benjamin, Walter. *Reflections*. Trans. E. Jephcott. New York: Harcourt Brace Jovanovich, 1978.

Breton, André. *Nadja*. Transl. Richard Howard. New York: Grove Press, 1960 [orig. 1927].

Chandler, Raymond. "Goldfish." *Trouble is My Business*. New York: Vintage [originally in *Black Mask*, 1936].

Chandler, Raymond. "Red Wind," *Dime Magazine*, Jan. 1938.

Chandler, Raymond. *Red Wind*. Cleveland/New York: The World Publishing Company, 1941.

Chandler, Raymond. *The Simple Art of Murder*. New York: Ballantine Books, 1972 [¹1950].

Davis, Mike. *City of Quartz: Excavating the Future in Los Angeles*. New York: Verso, 1990.

Didion, Joan. "Los Angeles Notebook." *Slouching Toward Bethlehem*. New York: Dell Publishing, 1961.

Fair, A.A. (pseudonym for Erle Stanley Gardner). *Double or Quits*. New York: Dell Publishing, 1960 [¹1941].

Gibson, William. *Virtual Light*. New York: Bantam, 1993.

Hertz, Richard. Personal Interview, 1995.

Klein, Norman M. *The History of Forgetting: The Erasure of Memory in Los Angeles*. London/New York: Verso, 2008 [¹1997].

Longstreth, Richard. *Markets in the Meadows: Los Angeles, the Automobile and the Transformation of Modern Retail Development, 1920–1950* [manuscript, 1994].

Robbe-Grillet, Alain. *The Erasers*. Trans. Richard Howard. New York: Grove Press, 1964 [¹1953].

Sartre, Jean-Paul. "American Cities." *Literary and Philosophical Essays*. Trans. Anne Michelson. New York: Collier Books, 1962 [orig. 1955]. 114–125.

7. "The Morgue: Fifty Ways to Kill a Man"
A compilation of graphic newspaper reports on murders in Los Angeles that served as a backdrop to Molly's story

Norman M. Klein

L.A. reporters in the fifties had a special fondness for very unlikely murders, those with existential plot twists. The more senseless, accidental – inexplicable – the better. Murder weapons were fired by mistake. Victims egged their murderers on. The literary style was unusually ripe, often comical, like crime melodrama on the radio; or perhaps the mood on the crime beat.

In 2001, while researching for *Bleeding Through*, I found thousands of homicides at a newspaper morgue downtown (circa 1900–1965). They sat eerily next to stories on Rose Parade floats. Everything was stored just as the reporters had left them. One manila folder really caught my eye. It featured 212 of someone's favorite murders, stamped from 1959 to 1961. The tough guy humor was everywhere, truly a hardboiled style. Victims were "slugged," or found "semi-nude," as if at a strip joint. Gentle personal details were slipped in, to round out the existential irony. Anything to make the crime seem even more inexplicable. Often, tormented former GIs were featured, usually white Protestant, the guys who never quite got over it:

"Man Held in Slaying of Ex-Wife's Mate"
Lee H. Beatty was an El Segundo plant security captain. His wife, Dorothy, had just left him, and remarried. Beatty was overwhelmed, es-

pecially after his attorney warned him "to use extreme care" with Arthur J. Myers, his wife's new husband, because Myers "might go 'berserk.'" After driving Dorothy and their ten-months-old son Eric to the airport, Beatty received a phone call from Myers, who was asking where his wife was. So Beatty invited Myers to his home at 304 16th Place, Manhattan Beach. There, the two men chatted on the couch. Beatty then pulled a 38 revolver that was hidden under the cushion.

"Murder: Girls' Fondness for Beatnik Life Told"

Durella (Corky) Boyer was a seventeen-year-old waitress who had entered "the beatnik lifestyle." Her murderer and occasional boyfriend, Timothy (Timmy Boy) Vance, had recently been held, then released, on suspicion of armed robbery. Before settling in L.A., Vance had served in the Air Force, but had taken to the beatnik lifestyle recently (what the writer meant by beatnik is never explained). Soon after he murdered Corky, Vance was spotted by her former boyfriend, Szendre. The two men chatted for a while. Vance returned the friendship ring that Szendre had given Corky because she apparently "had asked him to return it."

The Black Dahlia murder (1947) clearly left a dark impression on reporters. They seemed on the lookout for stories involving decapitation. Elizabeth Short, known as the Black Dahlia, had been found with her neck severed almost completely. The murder was never solved. And often enough, these stories about dismemberment were strangely ironic.

"'Head in Bag' Victim Named"

"A 'bowling bum' sought in $17,000 burglary Wednesday was identified as the man whose dismembered body was found in a mountain disposal pit... Mosser's head and hands were encased in separate plastic bags." Police also discovered "empty canvas money bags." "Deputies speculated Mosser either was killed by an accomplice in the burglary or was taken by surprise by an acquaintance he caught in the act of robbing the safes and was killed to prevent him from identifying the burglar." Mosser's fellow workers accepted the latter theory. "'He never had any money, he seemed to live for bowling, and he spent all his time here, but he's never taken anything that didn't belong to him even though he had opportunities,' said Bob Cameron, manager of the bowling alley." "Mosser, an Air Force veteran, who came here from Ohio five years ago, had been working as a maintenance man," Don Godard, the owner of the bowling alley said.

"'As far as I know, he did not have the combination to the safe.' he added. "Godard said Mosser was an expert mechanic but had been fired earlier from that job 'because he was always going to sleep on the job.'" "Two rings found on the murdered man's hands were traced to woman friends – one, Joan Neese, 25, 8311 North Harvard Boulevard, identified the silver friendship ring she gave him a year ago... The other, a high school class ring, belonged to a former sweetheart, friends said..."

"Working in Vegas Casino: Head Mystery Woman is Alive"

"After police found a severed head, a brother and neighbors of Mrs. Dorothy Hamilton (53) identified it as hers. But days later, Mrs. Hamilton was identified as living in a Las Vegas apartment with her husband, William, also known as William Bryan Brewster. "Detective Chief B.J. Maltin, of Las Vegas, said that Hamilton had been booked as a fugitive on a check warrant from Fresno." Both Garden Grove detectives and Las Vegas detectives were flummoxed. Detective Mike Winger said "Mrs. Hamilton was pretty emotional, so we didn't show her the picture of the head."

"'Misfiring' Gun Kills Man in Marital Row"

"'I honestly thought there were no bullets in the gun, it fired and misfired so often,'" said the tearful Mrs. Teresa Brill, wife and murderer of Frank Brill. The running quarrel began, she said, as they left their liquor store after attending a wedding. They had been married nineteen years, but he remained insanely jealous. "'He treated me like chattel.'" "'But I loved him. He was wonderful when he was sober...'" So while the argument kept heating up, Teresa stood it for a while. Then Frank slapped her twice. She finally slapped him back. That somehow calmed Frank down, but the argument flared up yet again, as the couple drove home. Mrs. Brill happened to own a gun, a .32 caliber revolver given to her by Frank.

"'When the quarrel started I put the gun to my temple and pulled the trigger. It misfired. Then Frank grabbed it from me and fired twice out the window... He tossed it back to me and shouted "you don't have the nerve to use it." I fired a shot through the floor of the car and he pulled over to the curb. 'I pointed the gun at him and it went off.'"

"Killer Rolls Auto Over His Victim" (apparently back and forth)

"Like any murder weapon, the car left identifiable traces. It has a broken tail light from hitting the fence, a cracked headlight from hitting the victim. And tire marks in nearby dirt."

Just below one homicide section, there was a 100-word article; filler at the corner of the page. It reported the words that a florist had painted on the back of his truck. The sign in red warned drivers who were too close: "Be careful. The next load may be for you." That surely gave the editor a laugh. Often, death has moments that are just funny, no matter how sobering. What this dark humor says about our true nature is anyone's guess. The usual answer is that we are laughing in the dark at our own fumbling and loneliness. Homicides back in Molly's day were often written as a kind of wake; by exhausted witnesses to crimes across the street; who needed to unload. Reporting crime made them wonder if any life can entirely add up.

I am reminded of one conversation that I had with Molly. According to one neighbor at least, Molly apparently murdered her second husband. But she never let on at all. One day, while sitting in her kitchen, filled with Depression era glassware, I asked if we could walk through her attic. I even silently wondered if I might find the telltale rope left by her second husband's suicide. Molly just said, "Sure." She was always the soul of kindness, or perhaps exhausted by her endless routine.

Her 1887 attic was huge but empty, except for a package wrapped in yellowed butcher paper. I asked Molly if I could open it. She said fine, adjusted her thick glasses. It turned out to be a package of Communist literature from the thirties.

"Oh, that would be my sister," Molly said. "She was the reader in the family." And with that additional plot twist, we left the attic.

8. Absences, Scripted Spaces and the Urban Imaginary: Unlikely Models for the City in the Twenty-First Century

Norman M. Klein

In Los Angeles, one can drive two hundred years a day. The slums remain – and will remain – in the perverse post-1960 twentieth century, like a misspent youth, a misspent modernism. The dingbat, stucco box, circa 1965, does not turn to slum gracefully, not like the brownstones and Victorians did; it simply erodes past the stucco down to the chicken wire. In the downtown area, the twentieth century is easy to find; it is a cordon in-sanitaire, like the death zone between the walls of eighties Berlin. The Growth Coalition [1961–85], a failed downtown plan for the most part, has left a ring of no growth around downtown itself. There is barely housing left standing on many streets west of downtown, and a prairie of neglect and confusion around the Belmont Learning Center, the ruin of a $200 million high school that cannot be completed, simply gathers dust.

In South Central, which is now increasingly Latino, much more multi-racial, the downward spiral continues. Erosion has not stopped [it accelerated with de-industrialisation after 1975]. In the storefronts, evangelical churches, the pawn shops, the lack of 'globalised amenities', there is a sense that de-industrialisation has left an absence from the last century. As a classic example, the Goodyear plant was turned into a flea market. Also, in the east and central San Fernando Valley, above Victory Boulevard, the decay left by 1970 is worsening.

Even LA as the city of circulation is grinding to a halt. Each year, on average, each freeway adds a minute of travel, particularly when it passes the wealthy districts [the twenty-first century]. Crawling along at ten miles an hour leaves more free time to witness what remains of impoverished LA, so little improved since 1970. In fact, I often advise drivers to avoid traffic by driving through poverty. Traffic runs faster through the twentieth century. Along streets like Santa Monica Boulevard or Melrose, you can see the line between the centuries: the over-dressed northern Italian restaurants, and the Starbucks, sure signs of traffic crawl ahead. The infrastructure of the twenty-first century is too fragile to handle globalised commerce.

At the same time, the nostalgia for twentieth-century LA increases, for a misremembering of its modernism. In the very expensive hills north of the basin, below the San Fernando Valley, a few well-placed real estate agents specialise in selling houses by Neutra, Soriano, Lautner, Koenig, by the Case Study architects [now very, very pricey and momentous]. Wealthy house hunters even arrive fore-armed, with pictures. They carry the twentieth century under their arms, photos by Julius Shulman circa 1950. They ask for a list of houses where they can live inside those photographs, inside the stylised lighting and ironic poses.

Much of the twentieth century may be in trouble, but it flourishes as a photo-literal memory. Certainly, the noir memory of 1950s poverty is flourishing. Dozens of film companies have turned downtown LA into a back lot of sorts. Buildings on Broadway, on Spring have for-lease signs on the second floor: "available for movies". The twentieth century as fetish, popularized by *Blade Runner* in the eighties [and perhaps fifty other films], has now become the standard memory of the city of the future as slum. Thus, the noir twentieth century is now an architecture of paranoia, a neo-gothic revival.

But now, after September 11, the next century finally has revealed itself. Its ironies suggest a future that is much more fragile, vulnerable, certainly to Americans. It will not be camouflaged by Prada stores and Vegasised and Disneyfied shopping cities. Beyond the 'visible' twenty-first century, in the citadels of power and poverty alike, the future looks much more feudalised, more balkanised and paranoic than many had imagined. We can now begin to excavate beyond the visible. Or should I say: layers from below have become much more visible indeed. They make one fact unmistakable – that the post-1989 world abandoned the twentieth century from both ends. It returned to a neo-Victorianism, even a late fundamentalist, paranoic medievalism. It slipped into a culture that precedes the Enlightenment, an Electronic Baroque, a new flamboyant [and repressive] catholicity dominated by corrupt media giants like News Corp [Rupert Murdoch], AOL Time-Warner, GE/NBC, Vivendi, Bertelsmann, Microsoft.

So we face a reasonably grim moment, compared with the glamour of the consumerati during the nineties. Clearly, that glamour will continue, but more in the spirit of Catholic fortifications in Moorish Spain in the fourteenth century. A vast ethnographic divide will continue to separate the centuries. And yet, without media, Osama bin Laden would not be widely known at all. He only exists on tape essentially, just as George W. Bush does, carefully edited moments, for global media.

In short, the global civilisation has begun to settle in. We see its monuments more clearly, its glitter, its brutality. Thus, we as critics, architects, scholars, urban specialists, can outline its features more inventively, more playfully. We have to humanise the furtive idiocy of it, speak honestly. This is a world that has more than lost its way. It is the best and the worst of all possible worlds, dominated by scripted spaces and social imaginaries inside a level of surveillance, top-heavy economic fragility and media feudalism that rivals the medieval papacy and the great caliphates. And yet, its possibilities are extraordinary. The next decade promises to be crucial. The challenges are breathtaking. Let me outline a few of our options, give a sense of how I imagine we can humanise them. Since I write so often about collective memory, erasures, and now also on simulation, I will concentrate on the city as imaginary, where two centuries are only a few stoplights away from each other:

Mature Suburbs and the Flaneur

Despite the lingering importance of the great metropolis, like New York, Berlin, London, Tokyo, Mexico City, LA, even what seems like a return to the urban core in these cities, the next century will not be dominated by urban centres – and yet it may visibly appear to be. Instead, the post-war suburbs have matured, and are now colonising the urban core. And tourism essentially suburbanises as well. Thus, residents are not necessarily returning to the buzz of the twentieth-century inner city. They are bringing the suburbs back downtown.

Thus, we are asked to become tourists in our own city. It is the victory of the *boulevards* over the *quartiers*. The boulevards were always about circulation and in-migration, like suburbs before the fact. The neighbourhoods off the boulevards were essential for urban life; and those will be very difficult to restore, certainly not essential to a suburb. I am not convinced that we, as an urban civilisation, even remember clearly what Paris in 1910, Vienna in 1900, Berlin in 1925, New York in 1950 were actually like, from day to day, in a quotidian sense, not simply along the boulevards.

Once again, we may remember more by way of photography. The photo memory concentrates more on crowds jammed at an intersection, at rush hour, at the theatre hour, crowds of children opening the hydrants for the Fourth of July, crowds stuffed into sweatshops, then jamming the street when the factory closed for the day. Something that 'looks' like these crowds can be reinvented, as a walk through an outdoor mall. But if you look more carefully at the photos, there is a difference. The mass of people on a Parisian street, or on Michigan Avenue in Chicago – circa 1900 – are not following a duck-imprinted path. They are milling. They are trying to get off the crowded boulevard as quickly as possible, to enter the part of the city they know more intimately, the cluster of streets where they spend 90% of their free time, the microclimates that are the heart of urban life. When they die, the boulevards fail.

We should remember that flaneurs were dawdlers on the boulevards – no direction, no plan. Flaneur was a derogatory term in nineteenth-century Paris. In illustrations, flaneurs are idlers in a daze; they are not deeply aware of what spins around them. They are walking as if in a state of hibernation – thus Baudelaire's ironic, decadent praise for the flaneur. We would do well to not recreate our fantasy misrememberings of the flaneur. Their world was reinvented as 'ruin' by Walter Benjamin. Now the flaneur is a consumer hibernating between purchases, an aesthete drifting through the streets. But is this another symptom of our malaise more than Baudelaire's ennui?

In a hundred other ways, cinema, television, the Internet reinforce that sense of walking in our sleep; or is it the sleep of reason, as we pretend that cities were simply about drift and shopping. On the other hand, the advanced, metropolitanised suburb clearly has matured considerably. I have watched the Media Centre area of Burbank evolve since it was first overhauled in 1989, around the time that Old Pasadena emerged, as well as the newly remodelled Santa Monica Promenade. These are now essentially the downtown centres, not only for suburban areas but for hundreds of thousands of people. Burbank calls itself "the Media Centre of the World", and it may be at that: home to Disney, Warner Brothers, NBC and over 700 media companies, the heartland for over $2 billion of media business annually in the eastern end of the San Fernando Boulevard. Burbank now hires far more than its population [100,316]. It is considerably beyond the bedroom community. I can see businesses chains from centres like Burbank and Old Pasadena filter through the Basin urban core.

Now let us translate this into social imaginaries, places that never existed but are remembered anyway:

Mediated Cities

As if at a studio in Burbank, an imaginary city is assembled by a team of movie researchers to identify how a 'mediated' city looks in 2002. The facts of 2002 have little relevance here, nothing of the mature suburb in the myth. Only the industrial city can serve as legend. The team studies hundreds of films, made from 1926 onwards, beginning with Lang's *Metropolis* and Vidor's *The Crowd*. In the first four hundred examples, two imaginary urban plans [topologies] reappear the most often:

1. the metropolis as vertical, like a layer cake, or sedimentary rock, more suitable for epic stories, for allegories like *Blade Runner*, *Fifth Element*, *Akira*;

2. the city as horizontal, like the circulation of the crowd, or the chase to murder – more deep focus tracking, like concentric rings running sideways. This is clearly more suitable for films noirs.

During the noir film era, from about 1944 to 1958, the horizontal imaginary city evolves into a complex grammar. That grammar owes a lot to the way New York is misremembered in Los Angeles [just as Lang's *Metropolis* is New York misremembered in Berlin]. During the twenties, LA/NY appears on New York streets at LA movie-studio lots. By the sixties, it has been twisted into hundreds of Expressionist variations. The central twist are its 'zones of death', locations where poverty and crime coexist under low key lighting, grim tracking shots and low ceilings. As the other side of the coin, wealthy and ruthless people hover above these zones of death, on hill sides, like predators.

By 2002, this contrast between zones of death and hillside views [the predators, what I call "grasshoppers hovering, about to attack"] is the skyline at night. To murder someone properly on film, you should have at least one shot of the grasshopper from the west of downtown. You also should descend like Dante from the hillside ["diamonds on black velvet"] to the circles of hell, as in the film *Mulholland Drive*.

Noir Broadcast News as Urban Planning

This noir grammar has become the standard way for broadcast media to dis-report the news, to generate a highly conservative, fundamentally reactionary vision of the world that finally covered up key information about the presidential election of 2000, the Enron scandal, the War on Terrorism, the anthrax attacks, Homeland Rule. But underneath the radar – that nasty phrase – we peek into another kind of madness: the city and the public space as it really is. What we see is outside the frame of the cinematic city. Outside the frame is the fact itself, from the real sociology of cities like Los Angeles or Berlin, to the price that Americans are about to pay fiscally and politically for this new kind of war.

Of course, noir reportage has always been a mode of distraction. Lately, I have been researching movie clippings of murders in 1959, about amnesiacs screaming for help, and a trend toward decapitated women victims – very much like hard-boiled fiction, or Film Noir. Now that distraction has become national presidential policy, and CNN, Fox, CNBC policy as well, on behalf of global media. Blind faith is our new credo.

So 2002 shows us a noir scenography as our national vision. We have extended this noir staging into national obsession with surveillance as well, evident earlier on survival shows, on the Web, on talk shows of all sorts. But now it is the credo at airports and office towers.

One wonders how this architecture of paranoia will be reflected in the scripted spaces of the future. Will themed streets be monitored like warehouses? Clearly, the borderless, globalised heroic era of unrestricted capitalism simply will not work, even for global corporations. We are witnessing the end of the comfort zone, certainly in the United States. And of course, it is not the fear of terrorism that frightens me the most; it is the emergence of American feudalism.

After all, the cinematic city often has suggested a dissolving identity, particularly in films like *The Matrix* or *Dark City*, about cyborgs and cybots without any unconscious at all, the post-Freudian, even post-Lacanian, and post-Deleuzian world, where no form of dialectical experience can survive. It is like a mental and emotional nuclear winter, so aptly expressed by directors like Lynch, but so desperately limited, so vacated, simply atmospheric nightmare without redemption, or even self-discovery. You struggle in the cinematic imaginary of the global city where you have no memory of your own, have no identity worth considering, have no inner thoughts that come from you directly.

That is the point of absence for us, where studies on alienation in the suburbanised and touristed urban core should respond. This non-dialectical cinematic city [very much the model that urban planning wants to redeem, and recover in many ways] has lost its connections to political and sociological 'realities'. It is mostly news as distraction, reality TV as reality talk shows, the recap endlessly repeating, like an airplane unable to land.

Bleeding Through: Layers of Los Angeles

I am currently in the midst of trying to engage these issues inside a cinematic novel/archive entitled *Bleeding Through: Layers of Los Angeles, 1920–86*. It will premier as a DVD-ROM and book at Future Cinema, a show curated by Jeffrey Shaw at Zentrum für Kunst und Medientechnologie [ZKM] in autumn 2002. A team of very gifted designers are deeply immersed in the project with me, led by Rosemary Comella at the USC/Annenberg Labyrinth project [who are co-producing *Bleeding Through*], and by Andreas Kratky [ZKM]. We are trying to imagine how to take this 'mediafied' city into a novelistic practice reminiscent of Balzac, but utterly consistent with the computer, with how collective forgetting takes place in cities as of 2002, with database as cinema, with the search function as a picaresque, covering 66 years of a fictional woman's life; and the possible murder of her second husband.

At the same time, this woman [Molly] lived inside the most famous 'zone of death' for noir cinematic murder – without ever seeing any of the movies. A researcher attached to our team has located dozens, if not hundreds of murders on film, all of them taking place on locations within the narrow three square miles where Molly spent her life. We are going through hundreds of photographs of the streets where Molly walked, interviewing many people who might have passed her in the street [including photographer Julius Shulman, who spent his boyhood nearby].

I want the erasures, the absences made by film to be self-evident. The cine-city that has grown in LA since the twenties, as if in a film lab, has now become the model for many urban plans: for the new promenade planned downtown, south of the Gehry Disney Symphony Hall, for the Hollywood and Highland project where the Oscars will show, for most of the metro [subway] stations that have been built, like movie sets, for the ambience of Old Pasadena, for West Hollywood's latest facelift, for the new 'artist' district on the industrial bowery near Main Street in LA.

This is strange for a city that absolutely isolated the movies and media from urban planning for eighty years [1912–1992]. There is practically no evidence that the freeways, or any aspect of urban planning or policy, took the movies into account all that much, or at all. There is even more evidence of deep resentment toward an industry filled with outsiders, 'wild' women, New York money as Jews – not a formula that Protestant leaders in LA felt comfortable with. But now, the movie industry is the model [even a brand] for an urban imaginary in LA planning that links news, cinema, the Internet and the scripted space of the entertainment economy. Indeed, the era of burbankising Los Angeles has arrived, with the integration of the media city with the mediafied space, as literally, as totally as industrial cities were once linked to factories.

Certainly until September 11, 2001, this mediafied city seemed magical. Its scripted [or themed] spaces were cathedral monuments to the 'new, improved' class structure brought on by de-industrialisation, post-colonial mis-investments, transnational economic blocs, and digital, cybernetic controls, along with overfed NASDAQ [e-business] monsters, and mega-merger super corporations. They were the realisation of all that NATO had promised before the wall went down, more like *arc de triomphes* than pharaonic pyramids.

Now that glow is gone [though the monuments are still there, and many more on the way, up to a hundred more museums in construction or retrofit, as I write this]. Will the easy-listening mood of these ergonomic, themed mega-structures continue? The myths of uncontrolled global capitalism have been challenged. A new wave of government controls are about to be added in the US, mostly at airports and at the borders, but also at oil drilling sites, for 401K pension plans [at companies like Enron], for the mail, for social security and so on. Even the Bush administration, so committed to no oversight at all by government on business, has to respond, particularly since the Vice President in particular may be compromised by talks he held with Enron.

The instantaneous, anonymous experience – whistling through airports, freeways, the Internet – is indeed over. And with that, these monuments, and the imaginary cities they respond to, take on a more ferocious aspect. They are more clearly honouring the separation of the classes. They look even more like the twenty-first century walking backward like a crab, to fortified cities of the seventeenth century. We finally realise as a civilisation that the barbarian, noir city – where poverty is isolated, outside the themed urban/suburban space – is not at all another century. It is the true face of our own decay and confusion, our economic fragility, our new modes of alienation.

Is it true that the global economy has widened the gulf between rich and poor to levels that resemble the fifteenth century? Have we truly slipped to centuries before the Enlightenment? Certainly we have in Afghanistan. The new lessons are clear enough: The transparencies of the nineties – that globalised fetish for 'smart' design – looks flat suddenly, compared to the alienated paradoxes of our civilisation in 2002. The last few years have shifted the socio-cultural agenda, despite all the controls exercised by global media and WTO and Bushist manipulation. Despite how conservative the moment looks, new modes of engagement are inevitable, in urban planning, and hopefully in many areas of the culture. We may indeed have to confront the urban core as more than the next step for mature suburbanisation. We may finally understand how to drive two hundred years a day, in architectonic work across the media and across the street.

9. Interview with Norman M. Klein: *Bleeding Through*, Media Evolution, Walter Benjamin, and American Politics (May 27, 2022)

Jens Gurr: Can you tell me about the original idea for *Bleeding Through* – how did it come about?

Norman Klein: It came about in stages. First, there was a Molly who I *did* meet, and in fact we even found a photograph of Molly and I had to leave it out, because I wasn't sure if we'd be sued. But then this all drifted into a corner and then I put it in *History of Forgetting* as the short docu-fable "The Unreliable Narrator" (rpt. as ch. 5 of the present volume), an obsession of mine. It is also conceptually an important part of that book. And then someone got wind of it and said, "Why don't we make a film?" So they made a film that I thought largely missed the point of what I wanted to do. It was called something like *10 Hours to Kill a Man*. It had lots of gaudy things to it, and was based on the idea of following this woman's life and all the different places in L.A connected to the idea of murder in the movies. Then, at ZKM [Zentrum für Kunst und Medien, Karlsruhe] Jeffrey Shaw was talking to me while he was setting up some project, and he had just recently rejected a job from the University of Southern California; and they were trying to see if they could change his mind. And so he said, "I'm doing this thing on future cinema. Why don't you do a DVD-ROM?", and he had an Australian accent, "DVD-ROOOAM", you know. "Why don't you use that film, you have a film!" And then I told him I was going to do it another way, from scratch. And then he persuaded USC to fund the project, and suddenly I was in business. They set up a team, and I still remember the first day, when they said, "Our job is to realize your vision.", and I realized this doesn't happen twice. So I invented the rhythm and the story while the archive and interface were being developed. Then I took the summer off to write a novella. And then, again very quickly, it came out in the late Fall, in an exhibition called "Future Cinema" – and then finally in a box set including the book and the DVD. So it happened in stages, in that pinball way. What certainly helped was that there was a tremendous amount of enthusiasm then in "interactivity", as they called it.

Jens Gurr: I was going to ask you about the media-historical moment of 2002/2003 anyway – that and then your views on interactivity now, almost 20 years later. It seems that there was much more enthusiasm then about the possibilities of digital media, more belief in the liberating potential of non-linearity in interactive media. You said in an earlier discussion that the arbitrariness of the interface, which brings the material up randomly from a database, and the resulting non-linearity, the fact that you're unable to retrace your own steps through the material – if you move three images to the left and then three to the right, you don't even end up with the same image – that all that was not as central to you in how you envisioned *Bleeding Through* as it was to your collaborators.

Norman Klein: No, no, it wasn't!

Jens Gurr: And in an essay from 2007 we also have in this new edition (ch. 3, "Spaces Between"), you even slightly dismissively speak of "clicking and clacking" (Norman laughs). Can you tell me how you feel about that now?

Norman Klein: I feel the same way. But now everyone agrees with me – they're fed up with clicking and clacking as a high aesthetic. They'd rather talk to the machine like a clerk at the store, and let the machine do it. At first, the feeling was that interactive surprises were almost a literary alternative or a mediafied alternative to traditional narrative. This was very much a late modernist idea, from the eighties forward, even the

sixties. And there are many, many versions of setting up data stories that way – choose your own adventure kind of things, and there must have been 30 or 40 festivals around the world dedicated to it; there was a lot of money going in; the University of Southern California was given millions of dollars to develop projects that would work like this and that's how I got connected – it was called "The Labyrinth Project." And there were also anthologies about it, first person, second person, and so on, and, of course, identifying it with games to a large extent. But the enthusiasm was largely somewhat confused, because the argument was almost something like: since it doesn't tell a story, that's even *better* than a story. Well, no. I decided I wanted to be more archival, partly because of my obsession with Benjamin, but also my obsession with archive and that it should take the "spaces between" that are supposed to be random and that they're narrative. And I've recently spoken with some people who do props for Warner Brothers. I spent the whole day yesterday looking for props for some project and they said, "Oh, that's what we do all the time: we set up an object that has some narrative hook to it. And the audience doesn't know what it is, but they feel it." So this doesn't have to be some kind of late-modernist Robbe-Grillet type of experiment; it could be a mode of narrative that is in fact quite pleasant. Throughout the nineties, a great many experiments with interface and cities were featured, in the arts and in architecture. I loved those, especially the work of Joachim Sauter. I wish more of that had continued. Now, what's happened since, unfortunately, in some ways, is that the early experiments as to how you might set up archival distancing and the role of the viewer and what the programming might say, of how a story like that can use layers, has almost lost out, and more and more, this kind of work is simply video narrative; so you might say, the three-act video structure similar to film structure has won out. You know, even games are more and more looking like movies. So this was a moment when it wasn't entirely sure that this wasn't another mode of narrative or dis-narrative and there was a lot of money behind it, and then by 2010, 2012, 2015, it began to dissolve and people realized that there's nothing more boring than clicking all the time. Don't get me wrong: I'm delighted with the interface for *Bleeding Through*, which perfectly reflected urban design and fictional strategies from that era. It appeared in dozens of festivals, won awards and even some twenty years later is still very appealing! I'm just not sure the randomness and non-linearity do very much for *Bleeding Through*.

Jens Gurr: So the non-linearity wasn't really central to what you had in mind?

Norman Klein: Absolutely not! No, I was quite convinced that the mental pictures you make are the powerhouse of all narrative. What you leave out. You play with the absences, so I felt there was a long definition of narrative that could easily include this interactive function.

Jens Gurr: What about the gaps and leaps? My sense is, if you had the same material that you have on the original *Bleeding Through* DVD in, say, a 90-minute documentary film where someone sits there for 90 minutes and gets the same kind of material thrown at them, then that would be less activating, less radical in effect in contrast to the interactive DVD, where you explore the material yourself.

Norman Klein: I agree; the spaces between fascinate me. I'm quite convinced there's something to what I call 'archiving' as a verb. It's a form of storytelling. Both you and I have roots somewhere in picaresque fiction going back many centuries. And we both understand how often there are gaps left in these picaresque novels. We find the character years later, with one leg missing. Something else has happened in between, but what, we don't know. Or take Virginia Woolf's *Orlando*, which makes these narrative leaps – there are so many examples of this, and we both find quite charming what Sterne called "the gentle art of good conversation". The gaps. The pauses. "So what happened in your second marriage after all?", and the person pauses, puts their chin on their hand, and then says something like "Well, it was a long winter ...", and then you almost *like* the fact that you don't know. And because I'm always interested in how people forget and collectively remember or don't remember, it's very clear to me that absences are as solid as a bridge, and in fact, you could say my real field is knowing what people are saying by what they don't say. And absences, which is so much what this technology was offering, should be studied still more in terms of narrative.

Jens Gurr: What about the leftist or radical *politics* of the non-linearity, this Deleuzian idea of the rhizome and that everything is non-hierarchically or anti-hierarchically connected to everything else, that there is a leftist political idea behind it? Does that make sense to you for *Bleeding Through*?

Norman Klein: I think it's connected with the way that entropy is understood in information theory: the more random something is, the more meaningful it has to be. But here? I'm not so sure the randomness is so very political in itself.

Jens Gurr: But you *would* say that the kind of subversive, bottom-up sort of anti-authoritarian view of the city, as opposed to hegemonic planning, is central to *Bleeding Through*.

Norman Klein: Yes, oh yes! All my work is about that. I mean, I often say in lectures, fish don't know they're wet, but they have premonitions. And so the study of how power filters through the material world, which is where Benjamin is the great master, is central here. To find modernism and modernity in shopping arcades, if you stop and pause: There's nothing more mundane than people buying bread in the shopping arcade, and yet it matters how the lighting works inside. So I think I don't see that as subversive exactly. I think what's been subverted is how people really live, the everyday nature of things, but I guess that's typical of someone who has always been identified as leftist, which I guess I have been. But then to me, the randomness is not essential to the subversiveness.

Jens Gurr: Still on the media history, the non-linearity and the fact that *Bleeding Through* came as a combination of literary text and material on a DVD: This was extremely innovative and greatly added to the appeal then. Now, for technical reasons, because the content of the DVD cannot easily be migrated to the web without re-programming the entire interface, we have a link in the book to a film that shows *Bleeding Through* being operated – and that is necessarily linear and non-interactive itself, though it shows the interactivity. And it seems there's a certain irony to this: I like the irony that when *Bleeding Through* came out, the non-linearity was radical, whereas now that interactivity is all over the place, we do this as a nicely conventional linear film.

Norman Klein: Yes! I guess the truth that was discovered in the last 20 years is that progress moves horizontally. We thought it didn't jump the rails, but it does jump the rails! All sorts of old horrible ideas are returning to the world, pre-modern ideas of land war in Eastern Europe, and so on, ideas of the nation state that go back in America to its colonial days and are unworkable; so why should narrative and media progress forward? It could progress sideways, even seemingly backwards. Take this idea that this new medium was not making us more reactionary and less progressive while it was providing all these wonderful toys. I remember between 1995 until around the time I did *Bleeding Through*, I was told many, many times, by people in media who will not remember they even said it (I'm an expert on people not remembering things) – they said: "Don't worry about the internet; it's too anarchic to make any money." I said: "Are you sure?" So the belief that something anarchic-looking is by definition a leftist step forward has been, shall we say, completely disproven by Cambridge Analytica, by people working with Trump, and by just bad taste. So we're now discovering the majestic idea that progress *can* actually move sideways and seem to even move backwards and still be progress, so this project is in a way part of that process. In his book *Dark Deleuze*, Andrew Culp writes about how Deleuze maybe wasn't such a progressive after all. So perhaps the collapse of the sign wasn't a progressive idea either, but worked very well with neo-liberalism.

Jens Gurr: What does that mean for the role of the viewer and the line between truth and fiction?

Norman Klein: You can't fix the role of viewer without bringing back Romantic Irony in all its muscular forms, from 1760 or 1790. As in a 1760 picaresque, the writer shakes the sleeping reader awake. It's a friendly nudge, a comical index finger. Regularly, as asides in the text, the writer interrupts scenes in order to chat with "Dear Reader". This is part of the story, not outside it. But what is our 2022 version of this old literary trick? The reader is not sleeping, sweats a lot, a more savage reader than in 1790 or even in 1990. The reader prowls furiously across social networks – armed with hundreds of ridiculous passwords, into rabbit holes less whimsical than Alice's. It is a war of nerves just to set up the boundaries and the code. What grievance culture version of Romantic irony does the Internet offer us? The Reader who is nudged gently now lives in a scripted space, not in an easy chair. This aggressive reader prefers the act of collusion, the myth of free will in a world of absolute predestination. So, the end result cannot be just clicking and clacking. It is too AI and unkind, a flattened kind of storytelling. Best to put aside the romance between digital screens versus printed pages. Who cares anymore? The reader corrupts our story; that is literature today. And so does the writer. I probably sound rather gloomy here. (Norman laughs). As for the line between fact and fiction, in some of the fictions I write, people don't know I'm lying for a while. Sometimes they'll talk to me later. As one example, I wrote a piece on an imaginary Freud: I wrote this novella "Freud in Coney Island", even though Freud really went to Coney Island in 1909. And someone contacted me, Zoe Beloff, a great video artist doing experimental video in the spirit of archive, and she said "Oh, did you know that there was a Freudian movement in Coney Island?". And I said, "Oh my God, there was a Freudian Movement in Coney Island!" And she did an art show and took my novella to help explain to people how it works.[1] And then I found out to my surprise, years and years later, that the version of Freud in that show was also fiction. She used my near fiction and fact to justify her fiction that there was a Freudian movement in Coney Island, so it's a fact-fiction-fact-fiction-fact-fiction, a kind of bubble effect, and media brings that out, but even if it's handled in some overly clever way,

---

1   Cf. Beloff's collection of short films entitled "The Coney Island Amateur Psychoanalytic Society Dream Films 1926–1972": http://www.zoebeloff.com/pages/dream_films.html.

this crossover eventually just creates a very, very flat version of story. And that's why a lot of games have very, very traditional story tropes. They're not the same experiments that you associate with literature, even with cinema; in the games, the formulas of character development have to be very, very familiar. And so it's all about staging; it's more like an epic form versus a literary form. There's something to be done with all of this, but historically, it's much easier for people to simply watch a movie. If I constantly have to "do" something and act like I'm the author, then you have to pay me, you know. (Norman laughs). Why do I have to be the author? I don't want to have to sculpt my own adventure, so that it turns out that the programming of the viewer is part of the problem. And then our sense of truth and lie has become much, much more effaced – the membrane between truth and falsity is just almost gone. And now it's become this political crisis as well. This was not so evident when *Bleeding Through* was made, but it's completely evident now – people can't stop thinking about it.

Jens Gurr: In the essay on scripted spaces that you wrote while you were working on *Bleeding Through* (ch. 8 in this volume), you commented on what has later come to be called "post-truth", or, more notoriously, "alternative facts" – the Enron scandal, the George W. Bush administration and the lies about Iraq, the craziness of reactionary media, etc. And 14 years later, Donald Trump was President – and what we once thought was the craziness of the Bush administration seemed like the good old days. So is that something you want to comment on with regard to *Bleeding Through* and media evolution?

Norman Klein: Not just comment on, but this year, I have to write on it – I have a book almost done that is centrally about just that. It's called *Vatican to Vegas: The History of Special Effects* and the first edition came out in 2004, so it was it completed immediately after *Bleeding Through*, but the notes go back quite a long way, and I'm working on a new edition of it and I have to change or update *all* the political references in it. I have a section talking about the election of 2000 as a special effect – just think of how much has to be added after Trump! And so I'm painfully aware of how this high consumer idea of making choices and the labyrinth of desire and so forth that was part of the internet and part of *Bleeding Through* and part of our political culture, has gotten poisonously dangerous to the point where it's the constitutional threat to what Americans call democracy. So yes, fake news and bullshitting your way through politics... it's gotten considerably worse, and I've been tracing this ever since.

Jens Gurr: Are you saying there is a continuity between "noir scenography" and national politics, as you commented on it in 2002 (cf. chapter 8 of this book) on the one hand and the present day and your recent, more directly political work?

Norman Klein: Oh my God, yes, in fact, that period, the period of 2003, is the end of an era of transition; the end of the Cold War, the beginning of having all these wonderful gadgets, was some false spring! What we thought was a renewal was actually a new kind of what I call the neo-feudal condition. The level of inequality is growing so ferocious, in the United States certainly, and even in Europe, despite the sense that Europe is more egalitarian than other places, and so all these things are connected to the story – there's a political, historical, sociological phenomenon tied into what *Bleeding Through* was trying to say about that era. Take the elections of 2000 and 2004 – and with each election in the US, it becomes more desperate. And then take Brexit – fact and fiction! I thought I was making a joke when I used to talk about fictions replacing constitutional facts. It wasn't a very good joke, because it was true, though back in 2000 I didn't realize how true it was.

Jens Gurr: But at the end, the reactionary media that helped George W. Bush and Cheney in 2000 ...

Norman Klein: ... and Trump! Oh yes! Same thing! I would always say a fiction is much stronger than a fact, it's stronger than a bridge because there are no facts that can change that sort of fiction. If you believe a fiction, it's a challenge to your belief, not to the truth, and I would say that as a joke. You know, and then everyone would smile, thinking, oh I don't do that. I remember telling people how it seems serious what happened in the election of 2000 and I got answers like "oh shit happens". I remember contacting various scholars, and I'd say "I'm grieving for my country. I think something's going to get much worse", and it did. So *Bleeding Through* in a way is a step along the way. I'm fascinated by the construction of history and the thin line between fact and fiction. But it's just that it's gotten much more tragic now that it's not a clever joke to make anymore. When you put an end to distinction between fact and fiction, you ultimately end the social contract.

Jens Gurr: There is that argument Mark Lila and others have made that the originally leftist idea that truth is a construction and depends on power, that everything is a fiction, everything is narrative, that we should speak of 'knowledges' in the plural, that that epistemological relativism basically helps the Trumps of this world – "fake news", "alternative facts" –, because they are just better at it, or more ruthless.

Norman Klein: Yes! I don't want to condemn speculative realism or Accelerationism, but think of 2016, 2018 or 2020 and it is not a very flattering period to look back at. And I'm part of it, because my work has been centrally about combining, mixing, even blurring fact and fiction. Now it seems very difficult to be that slippery anymore, so when you talk about these things – epistemological relativism, knowledges – now, you think about "alternative facts" and such dangerous nonsense, about the collapse of the American elections. And you think about the invasion of Ukraine, you think about what China's trying to do, you have these very serious questions. The whimsy, the cartoon-like quality, is disappearing fast. However, I still believe that nothing is more surgically powerful than humour! And this initial process of trying to find a way through this problem, so the irony of *Bleeding Through* is in fact a bit of an echo to the irony of what's happening to our world politics – I wouldn't make a big case out of it, very faint. Little, detached echoes. You need special equipment to hear it. But it was part of what I was thinking about, and I still believe that somehow this has to be turned around; the collapse of print, or whatever you want to call this era. And the fact that some of the early attempts at creating what they called "digital narratives" – this problem hasn't been solved. It has to be readdressed, because I think it's such an important question. There's no doubt that there was this worship of the role of the viewer and the death of the author that does parallel neoliberalism and the collapse of a lot of the basic infrastructure of culture and power. There is this, I guess, a Foucauldian argument, rather than a Deleuzian one, and then Benjamin, we have to go back to him, because he's in the shadows at all times. He is writing all of this literally in what Huizinga called "the shadow of tomorrow".

Jens Gurr: I was going to ask you about Benjamin. It seems we share a fascination with Benjamin. To me it seems that, though Benjamin is never explicitly mentioned in *Bleeding Through*, he is still a very strong presence.

Norman Klein: Yes!

Jens Gurr: In a sense, *Bleeding Through* is your *Arcades Project* for L.A.

Norman Klein: I've been obsessed with the *Arcades Project* since I first imagined Walter Benjamin's boxes of cards and Bataille holding them and how they survived the Second World War, and I was even called the American Benjamin at one time, and some people were going to fly me to where he committed suicide; what I would have said, I have no idea. What Benjamin taught me in particular was how the everyday ephemerality, the small objects, speak more to larger issues of power, the way things filter down. I learned about layers through Benjamin: with these layers comes the question why things are hidden, why people hide things. Benjamin became a master of the line between fact and fiction in a different sense, and so I was most certainly obsessed with him. And how we live comfortably in our skins, but don't. And then his story and his death were haunting to me. And then his experiments with montage writing and how to cross scholarship with literary experiments: Benjamin has been very central to me for a long time, but I never mentioned him in *Bleeding Through*. You've made me aware again of how central he really is to *Bleeding Through*. But I have a tremendous empathy for his struggle and for what he saw, and I think he was mostly accurate: the power filters through. To me, Foucault and Benjamin are not that far apart.

Jens Gurr: To me it's very important that your docufable on Walter Benjamin in L.A. from *The History of Forgetting* is part of the new edition (see ch. 6, "Noir as the Ruins of the Left"), because it seems that it informs much of what *Bleeding Through* does aesthetically. Would you agree that *Bleeding Through* is very Benjaminean also with its layers?

Norman Klein. Yes! I remember talking with Mike Davis, who was my editor then; he mentioned Benjamin, I think, in one of his books on Los Angeles, and then I said. "You know, I think I'd like to write about Benjamin." So I thought about the 1980s a lot and how reactionary it got and then I thought about the responses in the 1930s in the US and in Europe, and then I realized that Walter is an example of noir as the ruins of the left, the failures of a leftist position to hold up, in a very dark way, but in a deeply archaeological way of thinking; so to me, Walter Benjamin was almost like a noir writer. So I thought, why not have him show up in Los Angeles? Why should we let the incidental fact that he killed himself right on the border of Spain get in the way of a good story, you might say. So I took him there, and then of course the irony is, how do you make an *Arcades Project* about a city that doesn't seem to have any archival reality in the usual sense – and imagine this man who loved to take walks walk into Los Angeles – he would have ended up in hospital practically. So I love the idea of him there. "Freud in Coney Island" came out later, and I've done other counterfactual things since then. I liked the game between fact and fiction in thinking about the construction of history.

Jens Gurr: How about the notion of layering? You're saying that it doesn't really fit L.A. so much, because it has so a little of an archive. Benjamin has this notion of superposition, the notion that when you're a flaneur and you're walking through a space, somehow everything that ever existed or happened in that place super-imposes itself in layers that you're able to see simultaneously, even if what was there left no physical trace.

Norman Klein: Yes, I love that! And he's right! That method I use directly in *The History of Forgetting*. And I've done since! I had this old house, old for L.A., it was 1907 or 1908, and in the basement there were lots and lots of bottles of liquor buried and other things, and then I realized that it was a doctor's place and he didn't want people to know he was drinking. So I felt I was doing a Walter Benjamin excursion. And I found all around different pieces of the neighborhood that reminded me of Benjamin every step of the way. I felt I was working with him when I was locating the objects that speak to a period of transition that made Los Angeles what it then became. Yes, this notion of superposition to me is indeed very central to *Bleeding Through*.

Jens Gurr: You mean the bleeds on the DVD, when the old images dissolve into new ones taken from the same position, that that's quintessentially Benjamin?[2]

Norman Klein: Yes, and it happened by accident that the team came to work on it. You know who really came up with operating a lot of it – Rosemary Comella and Andreas Kratky. They would come back exhausted every Monday and I could never understand why they were so tired and then I found out that they were trying to match the photographs, because everyone knows that the past is in black and white, and the present is in color. So they just created this bleed and I thought it was a magnificent way of taking the working title that I already had, *Bleeding Through*. And *Bleeding Through*, of course, is a very Benjamian notion, superposition! With the different periods speaking back and forth to each other, that's the way it felt to me. So I felt that that was much more dynamic, maybe dialectical, if you want to look at it that way, but there's no doubt that Walter Benjamin taught me how to look at a street.

---

2   Several of these are to be found in the film version of the DVD: https://www. youtube.com/watch?v=dMX5xuuyIDQ.

Jens Gurr: We tend to think of Paris, or Athens or Rome when we think of urban layers, but then it seems that with a city like Los Angeles, erased so often, rebuilt and erased again and rebuilt once more, only in much shorter cycles, the idea that, as Benjamin says, "space winks at the fla-neur" and reminds him of everything that has ever been there, might also be especially pertinent. Take the cover image of the original *Bleeding Through* edition: South Main Street with City Hall as a fixture – and then the bleed from these old two-story buildings to the mid-century mod-ernist glass and steel block of the old Caltrans Annex, the building that housed part of the California Department of Transportation.[3]

Norman Klein: Yes, the later photo was taken in 2002 – and even that "new" building has long gone. The new LAPD HQ is there now!

Jens Gurr: So this is directly opposite the *new* Caltrans District 7 building, the Thom Mayne/Morphosis landmark. The building site for that must have been right behind the photographer when the photo was taken in 2002.

Norman Klein: Yes, and if you look at that image now, you have a sense superposition also works forward, proleptically. You almost can't help "seeing" what is there now. Our new cover image, which superimposes all *three* layers, is very much in this spirit.

Jens Gurr: Was Benjamin ever brought up in the discussions of how the bleeds were done and how they function?

Norman Klein: Not explicitly. But, of course, Kratky is German, and he's very, very well read, so it's possible he thought of that, but strangely enough, Benjamin didn't enter the conversation. I always felt that the spirit of what he did was very much there, but not explicitly. It's because he was earlier than that to me; he came even earlier. Benjamin was conceptually very much with me in the 1980s, not so much later, no

---

3   Cf. the essay in ch. 3 for these images and for further images of the site.

longer so explicitly. And the Benjamin I was obsessed with was more about archiving and how things are hidden and so forth, and he was, in a sense, my answer to the whole Freudian psychoanalytical idea of space and place. I found him a healthier way and I felt that Benjamin and Freud weren't that far apart in my own crazy reading, so I admit I had an eccentric reading of this magnificent structure, but I've been obsessed with archiving since I've read his stuff. And yes, I'm obsessed with a superposition that's a living imposition; it's not just architectural layers, it's actually a kind of breathing back and forth, and I do believe that that's a better reading of our modernity than referring again to Proust's Combray, and so on. I am so awed by those earlier achievements anyway.

Jens Gurr: Maybe we should bring in *The Imaginary 20th Century*? More than 10 years after *Bleeding Through*, you completed another multimedia novel. Can you talk about what was central to you with *The Imaginary 20th Century* and how it reflects your sense of media evolution? We talked about the media-historical moment of 2002/2003, when *Bleeding Through* was made – what about media evolution and *The Imaginary 20th Century*?

Norman Klein: How *The Imaginary 20th Century* started, actually not long after *Bleeding Through*, had to do with some early 20th-century illustrations of the future by French illustrators that were completely wrong, but also very beautiful – and I remember saying to Margo, "Don't you think we could do this better than them?" She said, "sure", so I said, "well, let's just do it: we'll do an imaginary layered book", but then it evolved very quickly into other things, and then I used some post-*Bleeding Through* thoughts, because it wasn't that far away at that time. The lead character would still be a woman, because it's so much fun for me to have a woman character taking me through the material, but she wasn't going to be this plain-looking, efficient woman who successfully runs this clothing business. She was going to be a woman who was overwhelmingly beautiful but depressed, and so she had the whole menu of men to choose from, but she always made bad choices; she always ordered wrong from the menu. So she would be an Anti-Molly in a way. I immediately decided *The Imaginary 20th Century* would be the opposite of *Bleeding Through* in other ways, too: *Bleeding Through* basically only has three square miles in L.A. as its universe, so I decided *The Imaginary 20th Century* would have the entire Euro-American world of the early 20th century and including some continents that didn't even exist, and so it was large and much more epic than a kind of modern tale, and so we went back to a picaresque form and then began from there. But the Harry Brown character that I use at the center of *The Imaginary 20th Century* does in fact already appear in *Bleeding Through*, where he's a customer. So there *is* this connection, but it's almost like trying to take it one step further. *Bleeding Through* has a quality of a kind of instantaneity of a sketch, and this one is obviously much broader and playful in a different way, and in fact it's been set up so that it never ends; I write new chapters whenever I want; I wrote a new chapter last week. And there'll be a new edition of it, so it has a different quality, but it was using everything we learned from *Bleeding Through*. Most of all, it was not stochastic at all; it was even more extreme in its idea of narrative. *Bleeding Through* has a stochastic quality, and you can't figure out how to get back and reatrace your steps. But for *The Imaginary 20th Century*, we tried stochastic methods and we just got rid of all of it; no keywords, nothing, so it is an attempt to move even closer to a kind of narrative. I see it as an advance and also bookends of sorts – the three square miles versus the whole world, but there are some overlapping characters; I guess there's a kind of a *roman-fleuve* attempt to it, however mediocre on my part, to have the novels tie in.

Jens Gurr: So does the fact that *The Imaginary 20th Century* has none of the "clicking and clacking", none of the stochastic procedures, does that reflect your increasing scepticism about the sort of non-linearity and the multimodal interactivity?

Norman Klein: Yes, we very deliberately didn't do that with *The Imaginary 20th Century*, because I felt that the scope was too large and the journey was stranger and so on, and then it's 2000 images rather than 1000.

Jens Gurr: You mean we need more guidance through the material?

Norman Klein: The discontinuities and the randomness are actually the real motivating force; I would argue that narrative is *about* randomness. During the last half of the twentieth century, there were too many inscrutable theories about how chance stops us cold. But look at us now: We're lost enough without chance. Besides, all narrative is a fiction anyway, a construction about the everyday. Chance merely exaggerates where we prefer not to go. Chance is just a leaky labyrinth, as I call it, but most certainly a narrative. The interface to *Bleeding Through* is a brilliant attempt by designers to negotiate how we half engage the facts of our life. But leaky labyrinths are not about mechanical stupor. The universe is cold and empty enough without our help. I mean, how many weeks of your life are a novel, does that ever happen? I've almost never had a week that was a novel.

Sources

Chapter 1, Bleeding Through: The novella first appeared in the booklet of the box set also containing a multimedia DVD: Norman M. Klein, *Bleeding Through: Layers of Los Angeles 1920–1986*, with additional texts by Rosemary Comella, Marsha Kinder, Andreas Kratky, Jeffrey Shaw (Karlsruhe: ZKM digital arts edition, 2003), 7–44.

Chapter 2, "Montage and Superposition: The Poetics and Politics of Urban Memory in *Bleeding Through: Layers of Los Angeles, 1920-1986*":   Parts and earlier versions of this essay have appeared as follows: J.M. Gurr, "The Politics of Representation in Hypertext DocuFiction: Multi-Ethnic Los Angeles as an Emblem of 'America' in Norman M. Klein's *Bleeding Through: Layers of Los Angeles 1920–1986*," *Screening the Americas: Narration of Nation in Documentary Film / Proyectando las Américas: Narración de la nación en el cine documental*, ed. Josef Raab, Sebastian Thies, Daniela Noll-Opitz (Trier/Tempe, AZ: WVT and Bilingual Press, 2011), 153–171; J.M. Gurr, Martin Butler, "Against the 'Erasure of Memory' in Los Angeles City Planning: Strategies of Re-Ethnicizing L.A. in Digital Fiction," *Selling EthniCity: Urban Cultural Politics in the Americas*, ed. Olaf Kaltmeier (London: Ashgate, 2011), 145–163; J.M. Gurr, "Critical Urban Studies and/in 'Right to the City' Movements: The Politics of Form in Activist Cultural Production," *Resistance and the City: Challenging Urban Space*, ed. Christoph Ehland, Pascal Fischer (Leiden/Boston: Brill Rodopi, 2018), 181–198; J.M. Gurr, *Charting Literary Urban Studies: Texts as Models of and for the City* (New York: Routledge, 2021), 62–75.

Chapter 3, "Spaces Between: Traveling Through Bleeds, Apertures and Wormholes: Inside the Database Novel": This essay was first published in *Third Person: Authoring and Exploring Vast Narratives*, ed. Pat Harrigan, Noah Wardip-Fruin (Cambridge, Mass.: MIT Press, 2009), 137–152. It is here reproduced from Norman M. Klein, *Tales of the Floating Class: Writings 1982–2017: Essays and Fictions on Globalization and Neo-Feudalism* (Los Angeles: Golden Spike Press, 2019), 257–280.

Chapter 5, "The Unreliable Narrator": This docufable first appeared in Norman M. Klein, *The History of Forgetting: Los Angeles and the Erasure of Memory* (London/New York: Verso, ^{2}2008 [^{1}1997]), 230–233.

Chapter 6, "Noir as the Ruins of the Left": This docufable first appeared in Norman M. Klein, *The History of Forgetting: Los Angeles and the Erasure of Memory* (London/New York: Verso, ^{2}2008 [^{1}1997]), 233–243.

Chapter 8, "Absences, Scripted Spaces and the Urban Imaginary: Unlikely Models for the City in the Twenty-First Century": This essay first appeared in *Die Stadt als Event*, ed. Regina Bittner (Frankfurt/Main: Campus Verlag, 2002), 450–454.

Cultural Studies

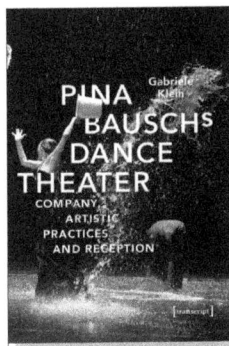

Gabriele Klein
Pina Bausch's Dance Theater
Company, Artistic Practices and Reception

2020, 440 p., pb., col. ill.
29,99 € (DE), 978-3-8376-5055-6
E-Book:
PDF: 29,99 € (DE), ISBN 978-3-8394-5055-0

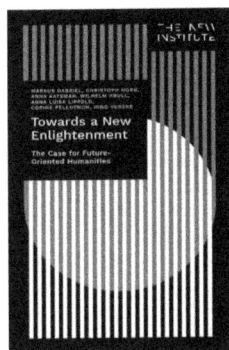

Markus Gabriel, Christoph Horn, Anna Katsman, Wilhelm Krull,
Anna Luisa Lippold, Corine Pelluchon, Ingo Venzke
**Towards a New Enlightenment –
The Case for Future-Oriented Humanities**

October 2022, 80 p., pb.
18,00 € (DE), 978-3-8376-6570-3
E-Book: available as free open access publication
PDF: ISBN 978-3-8394-6570-7
ISBN 978-3-7328-6570-3

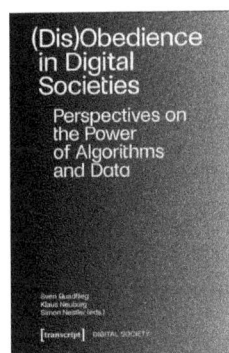

Sven Quadflieg, Klaus Neuburg, Simon Nestler (eds.)
(Dis)Obedience in Digital Societies
Perspectives on the Power of Algorithms and Data

March 2022, 380 p., pb., ill.
29,00 € (DE), 978-3-8376-5763-0
E-Book: available as free open access publication
PDF: ISBN 978-3-8394-5763-4
ISBN 978-3-7328-5763-0

Cultural Studies

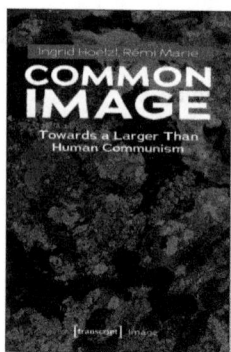

Ingrid Hoelzl, Rémi Marie
Common Image
Towards a Larger Than Human Communism

2021, 156 p., pb., ill.
29,50 € (DE), 978-3-8376-5939-9
E-Book:
PDF: 26,99 € (DE), ISBN 978-3-8394-5939-3

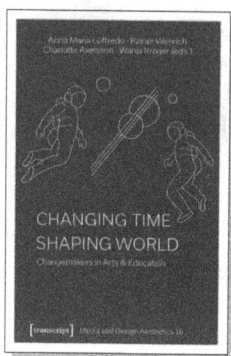

Anna Maria Loffredo, Rainer Wenrich,
Charlotte Axelsson, Wanja Kröger (eds.)
Changing Time – Shaping World
Changemakers in Arts & Education

September 2022, 310 p., pb., col. ill.
45,00 € (DE), 978-3-8376-6135-4
E-Book: available as free open access publication
PDF: ISBN 978-3-8394-6135-8

Olga Moskatova, Anna Polze, Ramón Reichert (eds.)
Digital Culture & Society (DCS)
Vol. 7, Issue 2/2021 –
Networked Images in Surveillance Capitalism

August 2022, 336 p., pb., col. ill.
29,99 € (DE), 978-3-8376-5388-5
E-Book:
PDF: 27,99 € (DE), ISBN 978-3-8394-5388-9

CPSIA information can be obtained
at www.ICGtesting.com
Printed in the USA
BVHW051955240123
657000BV00007B/74